A Handbook of Statistics and Quantitative Analysis for Educational Leadership

John W. Mulcahy and Jess L. Gregory

IES study
In Survey data ?
Wilcoxon Ranks Test
(-) Teacher effect score p. 48
Paired T-Test
or
Repeated Measures p 53

University Press of America,® Inc.

Lanham · Boulder · New York · Toronto · Plymouth, UK

⊖™The paper used in this publication meets the minimum
requirements of American National Standard for Information
Sciences—Permanence of Paper for Printed Library Materials,
ANSI Z39.48-1992

Contents

Foreword

A Handbook of Statistics and Quantitative Analysis for Educational Leadership provides an excellent reference for individuals interested in applying quantitative analysis to problems dealing with educational administration and leadership. The authors use their extensive experience in the field of educational leadership to create a text-friendly reference for both practitioners and researchers. Their insights into the realities facing the educational professional posits mathematical statistics as a context uniquely suited to addressing key problems in educational leadership. The traditional areas of descriptive statistics, sampling and measuring, hypothesis testing and test types are fashioned around questions specifically suited to the needs of individuals interested in educational leadership. It is this unique fit that makes the book both original and practical.

In order understand, from a statistical perspective problems in educational leadership, an individual needs to understand the mathematical meaning of the statistics involved, what relevance the statistics has to a given situation, how to apply the relevant statistical methodologies, how to obtain mathematical results form various calculations and the contextual meaning of the results obtained. This paradigm serves as the basis for the organization of the text. The authors give clear, careful and user-friendly explanations of the terminology involved in the various statistical analyses. They discuss the mathematical terminology involved, illustrate specific calculations (both with and with out the use of software packages), the meaning of the results obtained from these calculations and how to interpret the results in the context of educational leadership and administration. Straight forward and content relevant, the book provides a useful reference for educators interested in educational leadership.

While uniquely suited to statistical analysis of problems in educational leadership and administration, the clarity of the text will serve the needs of others. The book provides an easy-to-use reference text for many types of analysis involving descriptive and inferential statistics and testing.

The first three chapters of the book reference for many traditional areas of statistical analysis. They deal with basic statistical terminology, dependent and independent variables, parametric and nonparametric tests, sampling and basic ideas involved in hypothesis testing, levels of significance, Type I and Type II errors. Each of the areas gives a succinct explanation of the statistics involved and provides exercises which address the underlying principles in educational contexts. These areas include: curriculum supervision, duties of principals, design of university programs, census data and scenarios dealing with levels of significance.. These chapters emphasize broad concepts of statistical analysis.

The fourth chapter deals with a wide range of actual statistical tests. This section provides a number of classical distribution formulas. It gives details about the context in which one would use a formula, how to use the formula and why one accepts or reject a specific result. The distributions and related tests include: the Binomial, Chi-Square, Fischer's Exact Test, Chi –Square for Nominal Data, Cochran Q, Kolmogorov-Smirov, Wilcox-Rank, Krushkal-Mallace, Friedman, One and Two Group T-Tests, ANOVA, and Correlations.

The Handbook of Statistics and Quantitative Analysis for Educational Leadership provides researchers and practitioners dealing with administration and leadership a concise, clear easy-to-understand handbook for a wide variety of statistical analysis. It is a much welcomed addition to the literature on educational statistics.

Allen Cook
Professor of Education
University of Bridgeport
(Ph.D. Stanford University, 1996)

Preface

Why this "Handbook?" Just ask any graduate student, who has to run data analysis for: comparative, descriptive or relationship research questions. What statistical tests do I use to analyze my data? What are dependent and independent variables? Why are levels of measurement so important? Does my data analysis plan change when the levels of measurement change? How can the researcher avoid Type I and Type II errors?

We could go on and on with the questions. The bottom line is that to answer these and other related data analysis questions, the graduate student has to pour through hundreds of pages of text material in order to arrive at the answers. Wouldn't it be nice if all the student had to do was just to look at a chart or table to find the answers? Sure it would!

"A Handbook of Statistics and Quantitative Analysis for Educational Leadership" does just that. In less than one hundred pages, we have provided an easy "user friendly" text that will provide you with all that you need to know about statistical tests and their relationship to: Variables, Levels of Measurement, Levels of Significance and much more.

Just one of our data analysis charts literally condenses chapters in other texts. Simply "plug in" the appropriate data to SPSS or a related program and off you go!

The authors have a combined experience of over thirty years in working with graduate students and their data analysis plans. This "Handbook" was designed specifically to cut through all the jargon and get to the bottom line of what the student really needs - A comfortable, comprehensive and "user friendly" guide for statistics and quantitative analysis in educational leadership.

John W. Mulcahy, Ph.D.,LL.D.
Jess Gregory, Ed.D.
Bridgeport, CT; March, 2009

Acknowledgments

The authors gratefully acknowledge the 3rd. year Doctoral students at the University of Bridgeport for their proofreading of this work: Aresta, Claire, Christine, Heather, Marcia, and Wendy.

Chapter One:
Statistical Terms

Before computers, the most difficult part of statistical analysis was the calculations. Even with calculators, some statistical tests are tedious to compute as the amount of data increases. There are many computer programs (e.g. SPSS) that gracefully compute results, leaving one of the more challenging aspects of statistics the language and interpretation of statistics. This chapter is designed to clarify the differences between commonly confused statistical terms, and give the reader a primer in the language of statistics.

Descriptive Statistics/Inferential Statistics

Descriptive statistics are used to describe or give a clearer picture of the data. Descriptive statistics are used so often that they are sometimes overlooked as statistics. A student receives a grade in a class, or on an assessment, this grade is a statistic that describes how well that student mastered the content covered over time. Alone, the grade on the assessment or for the class may not give an accurate picture of how the rest of the class performed, but if enough grades were collected, a generalization could be made that would apply to the whole class.

Typically, descriptive statistics are used for that purpose; to make generalizations about a population based on relatively few observations. Consequently, this picture of the data allows the researcher to draw conclusions about the sample and draw inferences about the population from which the sample is drawn.

Statistical inferences are primarily

```
DESCRIPTIVE:
* Mean
* Median
* Mode
* Standard Deviation
* Variance
* Range
INFERENTIAL:
* Spearman Rank
      Correlation
* Pearson Product
      Moment
* t-Test
* ANOVA
* Chi-Square
```

Figure 1-1. Examples of types of statistics.

concerned with estimating properties of a population and/or testing a hypothesis about a population (Figure 1-1). Descriptive statistics include the collection, presentation and description of sample data. Descriptive statistics not only summarize the data but also show the variability of the data. Inferential statistics allow the researcher to test a hypothesis, and draw inferences; or rather make generalizations about the population based on the sample data. These inferential statistics use the effects of sampling errors to determine the relative confidence the researcher should have in the conclusions that are drawn based on the sample analyzed.

Population/Samples

When researchers use descriptive statistics, they are either using a sample of the population or the entire population. A population is a complete collection of anything a researcher wants to study. There are few cases when a researcher can use the entire population, for example a census, where every member of the population is studied. In those cases where the researcher uses the entire population they have eliminated sampling errors, no matter what the size of the population, and have values called parameters (Figure 1-2). A parameter is a numerical summary characteristic of the entire population.

PARAMETER

* *Summary characteristic of the whole population*
* *No sampling error*
* *Tend to be Greek Symbols*

STATISTIC

* *Summary characteristic of a sample*
* *Sampling error*
* *Tend to be Roman Numerals*

Figure 1-2. Summary of Parameters vs. Statistics.

It is usually too time consuming, difficult, and/or expensive to measure every member of a population. Because of this, most research relies on data collected from a sample of the population. The characteristic values calculated of the sample are called statistics. Because they are drawn from a sample rather than the entire population there is a sampling error, the chance that the sample may not accurately represent the population. Depending on the size and type of sampling technique, the sampling error can be reduced. In the media, the sampling error is usually listed as a margin of error.

Statistical Symbols

To help researchers more easily identify whether the information in a study is a parameter or a statistic, each has a different symbol (Table 1-1). This shorthand clarifies whether the data is for the entire population or from a sample of that population.

Table 1-1. Some statistical symbols for both samples and populations.

TERMS	SAMPLE (STATISTICS)	POPULATION (PARAMETER)
Mean	$\bar{X}$	μ
Standard Deviation	s	σ
Pearson Correlation	r	ρ
Number in group	N	n

Independent/Dependent Variable

In experimental design, there are several types of variables. A variable is anything that can have more than one value. A researcher tries to define variables so that all possibilities of response fit into a category; so the design is exhaustive. The opposite of a variable is a constant; it is something that does not change in the studied population or sample.

The most often mislabeled are the independent and the dependent variables (Figure 1-3). These are the two most important groups of variables, and go by different names. The independent variable is the stimulus or input, it is what is being changed or manipulated by the researcher. The dependent variable is the outcome; it is what is being measured as a result of the change in

INDEPENDENT VARIABLE

* Predictor Variable

* Experimental Variable

   o Selected Variable

   o Manipulated Variable

DEPENDENT VARIABLE

* Criterion Variable

OTHER VARIABLES

* Moderator Variables

* Extraneous/Confounding Variables

Figure 1-3. Summary of Variables.

the independent variable. They can be thought of as a cause and effect relationship, where the independent variable causes a change in the dependent variable.

In a non-experimental study, the independent variable is sometimes called the predictor variable. If the research is experimental, the independent variable may be called the experimental variable which may be a manipulated variable, or a selected variable. If the researcher selects a variable that already exists, it is referred to as a selected variable and if the researcher creates the variable it is referred to as a manipulated variable.

Dependent variables in non-experimental research may be referred to as criterion, as they are generally standards by which things are measured. In the non-experimental study comparing a student's grade point average (GPA) to their score on a standardized test such as the scholastic aptitude test (SAT) or Connecticut academic performance test (CAPT), the GPA is the standard by which the test's validity may be measured. It would be expected that students with high GPA's would have higher scores on the standardized tests, and therefore the GPA is the predictor of the criterion of SAT or CAPT score.

In addition to independent and dependent variables, there may also be moderating variables and confounding variables. A moderating variable is a secondary independent variable that is identified and measured because the researcher believes that it may affect the relationship between the independent and dependent variables. A confounding variable, also called an extraneous variable is an independent variable that is beyond the control of the researcher but may have unintended effects on the dependent variable.

Exercise 1.

Identify the type and number of variables in the following examples.

1. **Principal leader behavior: It's impact upon teacher job satisfaction.**

2. **Principal leader behavior: It's impact upon teacher job satisfaction and teacher morale.**

3. **Role ambiguity and role overload – their impact upon teacher job satisfaction and teacher morale.**

Independent/Dependent Groups

In order to correctly identify the statistical procedures to employ with a set of data, a researcher must know whether the data are from independent or dependent groups. An independent group has members that are completely separate. They are not connected with members of another group. The selection of one person or subject does not influence the selection or characteristics of another subject. If there is influence between subjects; the groups are dependent. A dependent group has members that are connected. There are two common ways that groups may be dependent: 1) The same person is used as a before and after or 2) Individuals are paired based on some characteristic(s) and assigned as a matched pair to two different groups.

Parametric/Nonparametric Tests

When a researcher goes beyond describing the results and attempts to draw conclusions or inferences about the data collected, they must decide whether to use parametric or nonparametric statistical tests. Earlier, in the discussion of samples vs. populations, the term parameter was defined as a summary characteristic of the whole population. If the researcher seeks to make an inference that applies to the population's parameters they would use a parametric test. Not all data will allow the researcher to make these inferences. There are very specific criteria that must be met in order to use parametric tests. If these basic assumptions are not met, the researcher can still make inferences about the sample using nonparametric tests. Nonparametric tests are not bound by the same assumptions as a parametric test; they are sometimes referred to as distribution-free tests.

In comparing statistical tests, a researcher must consider the power of the test, that is, the error involved in the test and the efficiency of using that test (Figure 1-4). Each of these components has value, and it is up to the researcher to determine how to weigh each component. The test a researcher chooses may be due to the sample size, as sample size may be determined by the costs involved in

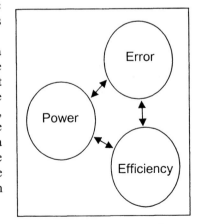

Figure 1-4. Factors that influence a choice of statistical test.

collecting the sample both in terms of money and time.

The errors involved in the statistical analysis can be related to the size of the sample, but are also connected to the level of significance the researcher chooses and the test itself. The level of significance is the α level, the probability that the results are not due to the variable you are testing. The other source of error, β, is the likelihood that the null hypothesis was rejected when it shouldn't have been, this is beyond the control of the researcher. The power of a statistical test is $1-\beta$, the probability that the researcher will reject the null hypothesis when it should be rejected.

Once the researcher has determined an acceptable α level and an acceptable β risk, they then must choose a test that can give them the efficiency they require. Efficiency is the comparison of the sample size that the parametric test requires compared to the sample size of the equally powerful nonparametric test. If the data will permit the use of either parametric or nonparametric tests (discussed later), the factors of power, error and efficiency are important considerations.

Exercise 2.

What factors would be involved in choosing a test in the following scenarios?

1. A curriculum supervisor is considering a new reading program, there are 12 schools in the country that are using the program. The school board is resistant to change without evidence.

2. A district is looking for a new principal for their middle school. The staff wants to be consulted as they believe that the principal's leadership style affects student achievement on standardized tests.

3. A private university is looking to start requiring another course before a student is eligible for a degree. The course has run for 6 years, both fall and spring. A staff member wants to see if the course has an impact on success after graduation.

Parametric Tests

Tests, from which inferences can be applied to parameters of the population, can only be applied when certain conditions or assumptions are met. The most basic of these assumptions is that the population is normally distributed, and that the data collected is also normally distributed. The sample tested should be drawn randomly from the population, and the data collected should be at the interval or ratio level of measurement. Additionally, the variances of the sample tested and of the population should be equal. As parametric tests tend to be more powerful, they should be used when the preceding assumptions are met.

Nonparametric Tests

Nonparametric tests do not require the same assumptions be met as their parametric counterparts (Table 1-2). There are no stipulations regarding the parent population, and tend to be easier to apply than parametric tests. While it may appear that nonparametric methods are wasting information by assigning ranks instead of using the actual value of the variable, the nonparametric tests tend to be only slightly less efficient than the parametric counterpart. In fact, if the assumptions required by parametric tests can not be met, the nonparametric test is actually more powerful.

Table 1-2. Assumptions of Parametric vs. Nonparametric Tests.

Parametric Tests	*Nonparametric Tests*
❈ Normal Distribution	❈ Distribution is Skewed
❈ Sample is Representative	❈ Sample Size is Small
❈ Data are at least Interval Level	❈ Data are Nominal or Ordinal
❈ Equal Variances	❈ Unequal Variances

Normal Distribution/Skewed Distribution

One of the major assumptions of parametric tests is that the data are normally distributed. The normal curve is based on the normal probability distribution. This distribution allows predictions to be made based where a value falls in the area under the curve. The normal curve has the mean, median and mode at its center and a symmetrical distribution extending on either side (Fig. 1-5). The total area under the curve is equal to 1.001, so that the probability that the value falls under the curve is 100%. When a value is

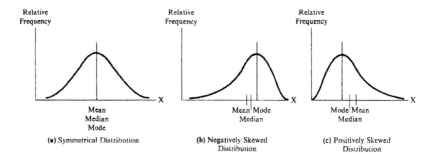

Figure 1-5. Positional comparisons of the three measures of central tendency for symmetrical and skewed frequency distributions.

chosen on the x-axis, the probability that a value will be higher or lower than that value is determined by the area under the curve. In the above curve (a) there is a 50% chance that a value will be above or below the mean, as the mean is bisecting the area under the curve. In curve (c), there is a greater portion of the area under the curve to the left of the mean, so it is more likely that a value will be below the mean than there is that it will be above. Figure 1-5 illustrates possibilities when there is one peak in the distribution, but this is not always the case. There are instances when there is no peak in the distribution, where the frequency is essentially the same for all values of x, this is called a flat distribution, and can result from a comparison of variables that are unrelated like a person's eye color and their height. In this case, there would not be a peak in the distribution as it would be unlikely that a person's height has an impact on the number of people with a given eye color. Beyond normal, skewed and flat distributions, there are those cases where there are multiple peaks in the curve,

---

[1] The actual curve of the normal distribution extends to infinity at both tails, so the area under the curve is an approximation of 1.00. This approximation is an assumption used to simplify the concept, it does not impact the math used in the equations that will follow in this text.

they are multimodal. A common situation is one in which there appear two peaks in the data; this is called bimodal (Figure 1-6).

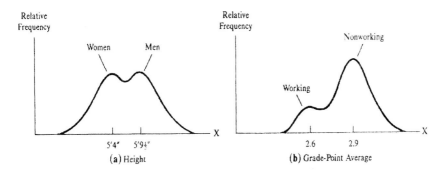

Figure 1-6. Examples of bimodal frequency distributions.

A bimodal distribution can be extremely useful if there are differentiating characteristics of the sample causing the two peaks. In the example of the height distribution (a), it would be expected that there would be a bimodal distribution, with a sample containing both men and women as there would be a range of heights for both genders, there would be a peak at the mean height for women and another at the mean height for men. The mean for the sample would be between these and not be a very good description for either group. In the bimodal frequency distribution of grade point averages (b), the two peaks would encourage the researcher to investigate further. The frequency distribution indicates that there may be a relationship between a student working and a lower grade point average.

A word of caution, it is very difficult to determine the nature of a causal relationship. One might look at this descriptive data and assert that working causes a lower grade point average, and that may be warranted, but it is also possible that students with lower grade point averages are choosing to work more to build career experience, and in that case the lower grade point average may be causing the working. There is no way to determine a causal relationship with descriptive data and even with further testing it is difficult to determine the direction of a relationship. (Which came first the chicken or the egg?)

Questions for Discussion

1. If a study cites a certain parameter, how is that different from a statistic?

2. Can a study have only a criterion variable? Cite an example that supports your choice.

3. Discuss a scenario where a researcher may sacrifice the power of a statistical test in order to increase efficiency? When might that be inappropriate?

4. If a distribution is normally distributed, would a researcher automatically use a parametric test? Explain your response.

5. A high school swim team is charting their results for the past few races. They are normally distributed. Olympic medalist Michael Phelps comes and swims with the team for a couple of races. If Phelps' times are much lower, how would that affect the distribution of results?

6. Sketch a curve for both scenarios.

7. Indicate the mean, median and mode on the sketches.

8. Discuss which measure of central tendency is the most descriptive for each curve.

9. Why is a positively skewed distribution called positively skewed if the bulk of scores are below the mean?

Chapter Two:
Sampling and Measurement

A sample is a subgroup selected from and representative of the population of interest. The data collected and the conclusions drawn are only as good as the sample from which they were collected. Even the most elegant mathematics can not compensate for a carelessly selected sample. This chapter will investigate the methods of sampling and whether conclusions can be generalized to a population based on the sampling technique chosen.

Representative Sampling

Any sampling procedure introduces a source of error called sampling error. Sampling error exists no matter how the sample is taken, but it can be by taking care to avoid bias. A biased sample is one that is not representative of the population from which it is drawn; this can be either due to a poor sampling technique or chance. Increasing the sample size will help to reduce the error if that error is solely due to chance. If the sampling error is due to an inappropriate sampling methodology, however, increasing the sample size will have no effect.

A slice of the pie cannot differ from the whole pie

Samples are used in research when the population to be studied is too large or inaccessible to study directly. In order for conclusions to be inferred to the population based on data that were collected from the sample it must be an unbiased sample. For example, if a food critic wants to review Annie's Apple Pies, then the critic must have a slice of apple pie and not peach. Further, it must be one of Annie's pies and not another brand.

Methods Of Choosing A Sample

When it is determined that a sample must be used to more efficiently collect data, the method of sample collection is the next decision to be made. Knowing that the sample, no matter how carefully it is designed or collected, always introduces a source of error, a researcher strives to reduce the sampling error by making the sample as representative of the population as possible. The larger the sample size, the greater the possibility that the sample will well represent the population. Even the US census has a sampling error—not everyone can be reached to survey.

There are several methods researchers use to collect samples:

- Simple Random Sampling
- Systematic Random Sampling
- Stratified Random Sampling
- Proportionate Stratified Random Sampling
- Cluster Random Sampling
- Two-Stage Random Sampling
- Purposive Sampling
- Convenience Sampling

Sampling questions:

✳ Is the sample representative of the population to which the results will be generalized?

✳ Is the sample large enough to inspire confidence in the results?

Figure 2-1. Questions to ask about a sample.

No matter what method of sampling is used, the researcher will never be certain that the sample and the population are alike, they can just do everything they can to avoid bias. All sampling protocols fit into two larger categories: probability sampling and non-probability sampling. Probability sampling techniques require that the researcher be able to define all the elements of a population and have access to all the members of that population. Only probability sampling techniques will yield a sample representative of the entire population.

Simple Random Sampling requires that the researcher have a list of every element in the population, and each element of the population has an equal chance of being selected. This is an example of a probability sampling technique. The selection of one element of the population has no impact on the selection of any other element of the population. There are two types of simple random sampling: there is simple random sampling with replacement and simple random sampling without replacement. Depending on whether the researcher allows for elements to be selected more than once, they would opt to replace items or exclude them from possibly being selected multiple times. To avoid bias in the selection of elements of the population, either a computer or a table of random numbers is used to choose from the population.

Systematic Random Sampling, also a probability method, requires that the researcher have a list of every element in the population, and each element of the population has an equal chance of being selected. Again, the selection of one element of the population has no impact on the selection of any other element of the population. The major difference between simple random sampling and systematic random sampling is that the researcher begins a simple random procedure, but then selects every nth element until the desired sample size is obtained. However, the selection of every nth element adds another opportunity for bias.

Sampling and the US Census

Since the adoption of the US Constitution, the government was charged with taking a decennial census. Until the 20th century, the government carried out an enumeration (head count) to the best of its ability. As the role of government activity in everyday life increased, so did the level of detail required in the census. The census bureau developed two forms, a short and long. The long form was sent to a sample of the population, and the results generalized to the rest of the population and a short form that went to a greater percentage of the population to provide an enumeration. In the 1990 decennial the combination of both forms missed 8.4 million Americans and double-counted 4.4 million (US Census). Due to rising costs, the US census bureau planned to survey 90% of people in each and visit a sample of non-respondents. The US Supreme Court ruled that sampling techniques could not be used for congressional appointments according to Title 13 of the US Code. This drew attention to the sampling techniques that have been used in other decennial censuses.

Discussion Questions

What are some motivations/ concerns related to using sampling with the US decennial census?

What are the historical arguments that led to the US Supreme Court ruling in 1999?

Do you feel sampling techniques should be employed for the next decennial census?

Stratified Random Sampling addresses some of the concerns in the sampling error introduced in the methods above. While like the other protocols in that this is a probability technique, in neither simple random nor systematic random sampling did the researcher attempt to make sure the sample was representative of the population, only through increasing sample size is the error reduced in those methods. In stratified random sampling the population is divided into subgroups and the samples are drawn from those groups, or strata. This is useful when the researcher is making comparisons among the subgroups, where subgroups have extremely different characteristics, or when there is concern that a subgroup may be unrepresented in the sample.

Proportionate Stratified Random Sampling adds yet another component to the stratified random sampling protocol to help reduce bias, and sampling error. In proportionate stratified random sampling, the researcher ensures that the sample and the population have the same proportions of identified subgroups. Proportionate stratified random sampling requires that the researcher be able to accurately measure the percentages of each subgroup in the population, but by doing so they can also collect a sample that has the same proportions of the population it is designed to represent.

Cluster Random Sampling is the probability technique used when the researcher can not design a stratified sample, but still wants to limit the possibility of an unrepresentative sample. In cluster sampling, the population is divided into clusters, and then through a simple random sampling technique clusters are selected. Once clusters are selected; any applicable sampling technique can be used to sample elements from within the selected clusters. This methodology saves resources in that it can limit the number of surveys or interviews, the travel costs or the resources required to gather enough information to stratify the entire population. Clusters are smaller and therefore allow the researcher to collect more information if they wish to use a proportionate stratified random sampling protocol. An example of this procedure would be when a politician wants to poll a large population, they would divide the population into clusters that could easily be contacted, and then randomly choose some of these clusters to survey.

Two-Stage Random Sampling is similar to the cluster random sampling except the researcher uses groups that are already defined, like classes in an elementary school, or departments in a company. This probability technique uses clusters that are already formed due to some characteristic and the researcher randomly selects from among the pre-formed clusters, and then applies any other sampling methodology. This procedure may used because it is more efficient as the groups are already defined, or because other methods of clustering can not be used.

Purposive Sampling is a non-probability technique, differs from the other methods in that the sample is chosen only from a group that meets a specific criterion (e.g. people who are color blind). This form of sampling limits the population to which the results of the sample can be applied, but is useful when other sampling techniques may miss the targeted population because it is rare or difficult to sample.

Convenience Sampling is the least expensive in terms of resources, but very limited in that is it subject to large sampling errors. This is the other non-probability technique discussed. In convenience sampling, the researcher uses the subjects that are readily available. There is limited attention to whether the sample is representative of the entire population, and the targeted population may have to be redefined based on the sample that is available.

Exercise 3.

What type of sampling would be involved in the following scenarios?

---

1. A curriculum supervisor is considering a new reading program, there are 12 schools in the country that are using the program. The school board is resistant to change without evidence.

2. A district is looking for a new principal for their middle school. The staff wants to be consulted as they believe that the principal's leadership style affects student achievement on standardized tests.

3. A private university is looking to start requiring another course before a student is eligible for a degree. The course has run for 6 years, both fall and spring. A staff member wants to see if the course has an impact on success after graduation.

Measurement

When a researcher plans a study they anticipate what type of information they are going to collect and analyze. If that information is numerical in nature it is generally referred to as a measurement. Formally, a measurement is any number or label that a researcher attributes to a specific item or occurrence. Because these measurements vary in level, they are categorized based on a scale of their complexity. Knowing the level of measurement helps the researcher choose an appropriate statistical test and helps the consumer of research interpret what the measurements represent. There are four commonly defined levels of measurement (from least to most complex): (a) Nominal, (b) Ordinal, (c) Interval, and (d) Ratio. The nominal scale has the lowest degree of precision. The ratio scale has the highest degree of precision.

Once assigned, numbers attain certain properties representative of characteristics that determine which arithmetic operations can be performed (Figure 2-2).

The Nominal Scale is the weakest level of measurement. This scale uses numbers as labels to identify or classify objects or individuals. When elements of a population are classified using the nominal scale of measurement, they are placed into mutually exclusive categories. The nominal level of measurement provides the researcher with a numerical way to identify information, but it does not allow for arithmetic calculations. The numbers assigned to race cars do not indicate the order in which they will finish, nor can they be averaged to describe the field of race cars, they are merely a method of identifying the driver of the car. The nominal level of measurement is most useful in comparing frequencies, the number of items that are categorized as such. Percentage data can be nominal when it is counting the frequency relative to the whole sample. If there are 50 people in a sample, and 20 are men, then the percentage that is male is 40%. In this example, 20 people were categorized as male, and 30 as female. For the nominal level of measurement, the measure of central tendency is the mode, the item that appears most frequently. In the sample of 50 people above, the mode would be female, as the frequency of people categorized as female is higher than that of male (30>20).

Level of measurement and mathematical operations

Nominal: Numbers on football jerseys to identify players cannot be added, subtracted, etc.

Ordinal: Numbers assigned to ranking, the hardness of gems, are based on a continuum, but they cannot be added or subtracted, etc.

Interval: Test scores can be added, subtracted.

Ratio: Weight/age can have all the arithmetic operations performed on them.

Figure 2-2. Measurement scales and arithmetic operations.

The Ordinal Scale is the next level of measurement. This scale gives more information than the nominal scale; it identifies and classifies information like the nominal scale but adds a dimension. The ordinal scale includes a ranking of information or objects in some kind of order. For example, if the scenario of the race cars is expanded, each car is labeled by a number and then ranked according to their qualifying scores. The actual qualifying scores are not kept, just the rank order of the cars. In this example and in any other ordinal situation, each individual is reviewed on the basis of a selected criterion and then ranked from highest to lowest. The ordinal scale does not offer information on how closely spaced the elements are, nor does it give information about the overall values of the elements, it merely relates one element of the population to another in terms of order.

When working with ordinal data, the most appropriate measure of central tendency is the median. While the mode is also an appropriate measure of central tendency, the median is more sensitive than the mode. To assess variability with ordinal data, the range describes the amount of variability and the semi-quartile deviation the index of variability. These measures are associated with a box and whisker plot of data (Figure 2-3).

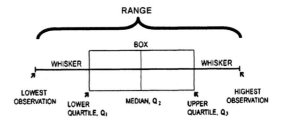

Figure 2-3 Sample Box and Whisker plot

The range is merely the difference between the highest and the lowest scores. The semi-quartile deviation takes into account the median of the numbers above and below the median of the whole set. The semi-quartile deviation is less subject to sampling error in skewed data sets. If the semi-quartile deviation is small the data are closely grouped, if it is large then the data are more widely distributed. The semi-quartile deviation provides much more information than the range alone. Together the range and the semi-quartile deviation can provide a representation of the distribution of elements for ordinal data.

The Interval Scale is the third level of measurement. This scale gives more precision and sensitivity than either the nominal or ordinal scales. Values on the scale are evenly spaced and can be compared, as can the differences between values on the scale. Scores at the interval level of measurement can be added and subtracted, but may not be manipulated through multiplication or division. The interval scale does not have an absolute zero. Revisiting the race car example, if car drivers were surveyed as to their opinions on a new system of making right as well as left turns in races with a Likert style survey (they were asked whether they Strongly Agree, Agree, Neutral, Disagree, or Strongly Disagree with a change to the new system) the data would be interval in nature. A score of 4 is the same distance from either a 3 or a 5, but a score of 3 is not twice as passionate as that of 1.5. Another common example of an interval scale is the Fahrenheit temperature scale[1].

The measure of central tendency that is most appropriate for the interval scale of measurement is the mean. Interval is the lowest level of measurement where the mean and standard deviation are appropriate tools for describing the distribution of data. With the standard deviations, the variance (square of the

---

[1] It is commonly assumed that any degree Fahrenheit has an equal value, that the degree between 33 and 34 is the same as the degree between 198 and 199. There are slight differences it the amount of energy needed to raise a substance one degree Fahrenheit, depending on where it is in the scale.

standard deviation) can be calculated, allowing a researcher to determine whether parametric tests can be applied to the data. Parametric tests can not be applied to data at the nominal or ordinal levels.

The Ratio Scale is the strongest level of measurement. The ratio scale contains all the properties of the other scales except it has an absolute zero instead of an arbitrary zero. Unlike the Fahrenheit temperature scale, the Kelvin temperature scale would generate ratio data, as it has an absolute value for zero. Temperature is defined as the average energy of the motion of the molecules in a substance; the Kelvin scale has zero set where all molecular motion stops. To determine absolute zero, scientists cooled gasses as much as was possible with technology, graphed the data and extrapolated the line to where molecular motion would stop.

If we look at our race cars, the times in which they completed the race would be ratio level data. The start of the race would be the zero point, and we could label, rank, and compare the scores. In this case, if one car has a time of 3 that is twice as long as 1.5. All arithmetic operations are appropriate for ratio level data, and like the interval scale, the mean and standard deviation are the most appropriate measures of central tendency. If the data meet the other assumptions of parametric tests, the parametric inferential statistics will provide the best results.

Table 2-1. Levels of Measurement Summary

Level	Scale	Process	Data	Some Appropriate Statistics	
				Descriptive	Inferential
4	Ratio	Equal intervals True zero Ratio relationship	Parametric	Mean Standard Deviation	T test ANOVA ANCOVA Factor analysis
3	Interval	Equal intervals No true zero			
2	Ordinal	Ranked in order	Nonparametric	Median Quartile Deviation Stanines	Mann-Whitney Wilcoxin
1	Nominal	Classified and counted		Mode	Chi-square Sign

Exercise 4

What levels of measurement are present in the following?

---

1. A curriculum supervisor is considering a new reading program, there are 12 schools in the country that are using the program. The school board is resistant to change without evidence.

2. A district is looking for a new principal for their middle school. The staff wants to be consulted as they believe that the principal's leadership style affects student achievement on standardized tests.

3. A private university is looking to start requiring another course before a student is eligible for a degree. The course has run for 6 years, both fall and spring. A staff member wants to see if the course has an impact on success after graduation.

Questions for Discussion

1. If asked to determine the color of shoe preferred by most adult men, how could a researcher collect the required data?

2. What would their sampling methodology be?

3. What are the strengths and limitations of that methodology?

4. What are some other protocols the researcher could use?

5. Why would those protocols be more/less efficient?

6. Why are the levels of measurement referenced in terms of strength?

7. Explain the relationship between the levels of measurement and the most appropriate measure of central tendency for each.

8. Why can parametric tests be used on interval and ratio level data but not on nominal or ordinal?

9. Propose a research scenario. What is the level of measurement for the independent variable(s)? What is the level of measurement for the dependent variable(s)?

Chapter Three:
Hypothesis Testing

When researchers strive to answer a question, they propose a hypothesis, devise a protocol and collect data as a means to draw a conclusion. Whether the data collected support a conclusion is due in part to the method of data collection and the nature of the collected data, but it is also due to the procedure used to test the hypothesis. Drawing inferences about a population based on the data collected from a sample of that population is inferential statistics. These inferences are drawn by testing hypotheses using mathematical tests on collected data.

Types of Hypotheses

Hypothesis testing is required in order to use a statistical test for inferring to the parent population from a sample. There are several types of hypotheses: null, non-directional, directional, and alternate. The alternate is not really its own class of hypothesis, but rather the opposite of whatever hypothesis the researcher states. For example, if lollipop preferences of 3-year olds were being studied, a researcher might hypothesize that 3-year olds will prefer red lollipops over purple. The alternate hypothesis in this case is that 3-year olds will prefer purple lollipops over red ones.

Alternate hypotheses are commonly referred to as research hypotheses because they tend to be stated in a very easy to understand format and represent what the researcher really believes will be the outcome. These are not generally what are tested. From a research hypothesis a null hypothesis will be formed. In the lollipop example, the researcher believes that 3-year olds will express a preference. Either the researcher has read something about 3-year olds, or has known some; or from this background knowledge they assert that red will be preferred. The research hypothesis states that there will be a significant difference in the frequency that red lollipops are chosen, and that red will be chosen most often. Note that by stating that 3-year olds will prefer red lollipops that there are really two parts to the hypothesis, one that there will be a difference and two that red will be chosen most frequently. The null hypothesis begs the second part of this. It stops and says that there will be no significant difference in the number of times red is chosen.

The null hypothesis has a pattern, or a stock format. If one were to research the relationship between hours of television watched and high school grade point average, the null hypothesis would read that there is no significant relationship between the number of hours of television watched and high school grade point average. Null hypotheses always state that there is no significant difference, or relationship or anything. It is the negation that defines it as null. The word significant here is referring only to statistical significance. Statistical tests are applied to null hypotheses and based on the results the null hypothesis is either accepted or rejected.

Back to the lollipops; if the researcher doesn't believe the null, that is perfectly ok. The null hypothesis is used out of convention, and like the statistical terms, it is the understanding and using conventional terms that makes it easier for researchers to communicate their findings. If our lollipop researcher does not state the null, but rather only states his research hypothesis, it is still assumed that he is testing the null. If our researcher tests 3,500 3-year olds from all over the country using a simple random method of sampling, and he finds that 1,850 prefer red, and 1,650 prefer purple, can he support his hypothesis that 3-year olds prefer red lollipops. Beyond that statement, how confident would he be in his assertion? Questions like this require statistical tests and can drive a toy manufacturer to change a whole product line, and example of how statistical significance and real significance can be related.

> **Hypothesis testing at a glance**
>
> *If the null hypothesis is rejected, the alternate (research hypothesis) is accepted.*
>
> *If the null hypothesis is not rejected, the alternate (research hypothesis) is not accepted.*
>
> *Never use "proved" or "disproved", since by chance alone the results may be incorrect.*
>
> *If the research hypothesis is accepted, it only says that the evidence provided by the study findings supports the research hypothesis.*

Figure 3-1. Hypothesis testing basics.

When our researcher chose and applied a statistical test he found that the results were indeed significant. The p value that was calculated was lower than the value he had set as benchmark; this means that he can reject the null hypothesis. This creates a double negative situation, where he rejects that there is no difference, meaning that his data supports that there is a difference, that he can accept his research hypothesis. Finding statistical significance does not prove that 3-year olds have a preference, it supports it. A researcher can not "prove" or "disprove" a hypothesis, rather they can only support either the null or alternate hypothesis.

Directional and Non-Directional Hypotheses are both types of research hypotheses. The research hypothesis in the lollipop example was that red was the preferred color of 3-year olds. This is called a directional hypothesis. Not only does it state that there is a difference in the lollipop preference, but also it asserts a direction for the difference. The alternate hypothesis used in this example was also directional; it asserted that purple would be preferred. A non-directional hypothesis for this scenario would be that 3-year olds will choose one color lollipop more than another. A non-directional hypothesis is more easily translated into a null than a directional hypothesis because it does not indicate that some event is more or less significant for one group than another group.

Another scenario might be whether gender affects the age a person earns their first paycheck. A non-directional hypothesis could be that there is a significant difference in the average age boys and girls begin earning a paycheck. A directional hypothesis would have specified the nature of the difference, for example, girls earn first paychecks at a lower average age than boys. From here the alternate hypothesis could take a couple forms: the genders could be rearranged, or the directional word "lower" could become "higher." No matter how the alternate is written, it must assert the opposite of the directional hypothesis. A null hypothesis for this example would be written: There is no significant difference in the average age boys and girls begin earning a paycheck. Notice how similar the null and non-directional hypotheses are.

Exercise 5.

Creating hypotheses.

A sports agent has just booked a hot new prospect. She has found a great left-handed quarterback who has superior agility, accuracy and distance. She wants to get this player a great contract as her percentage will be higher depending on the player's salary. Before approaching teams, she wants to be armed with research. She is comparing the quarterback ratings of right handed and left handed quarterbacks who have started more than 3 seasons in the pros.

What is a directional hypothesis for this scenario?

What is the alternate hypothesis?

What is a non-directional hypothesis?

What is the null hypothesis?

Levels of Significance and Probability

Probability and the Level of Significance are directly connected and at the heart of all statistical tests. Probability refers to the relative frequency of occurrence of an event over a number of trials, and the level of significance refers to the probability that a conclusion is due to chance alone and not due to the factor being tested. Both of these concepts depend on an understanding of the normal distribution. Before probability and level of significance can be more thoroughly discussed, a basic understanding of the normal distribution is required.

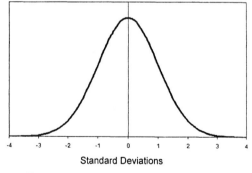

Figure 3-2. The Normal Curve

The Normal Distribution

The Normal Distribution is also referred to as the normal curve or bell-curve. The normal distribution is a symmetrical representation of data where the mean median and mode are all represented by the same number (Figure 3-2). The probability of a result is measured by calculating the area under the normal curve associated by a given value. This is a very abstract concept, but it is the foundation on which hypothesis testing is built.

Notice in figure 3-2 that the highest part of the curve is centered at zero standard deviations. This is the location of the mean, median and mode of this distribution. Unlike the skewed distributions in figure 1-5 there is symmetry present. The normal curve has very specific properties regarding the number of values found under each section of the curve. If a distribution of data is normally distributed, 34.13% of the values will fall between zero and one standard deviation. If a researcher includes both sides of the normal curve, then roughly 68% of the values will lie within one standard deviation of the mean. This range, ±1 standard deviation is referred to as the "Average Range" (Figure 3-3). There are two ways to interpret this, and both are correct: sixty-eight percent of the area under the curve is between one standard deviation above and

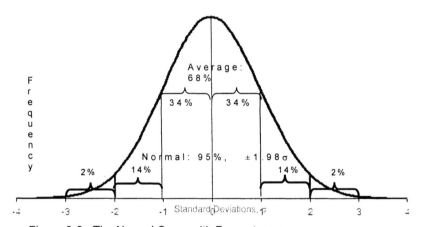

Figure 3-3. The Normal Curve with Percentages

one standard deviation below the mean, and there is a sixty-eight percent chance that the value will fall between one standard deviation above or below the mean.

If a researcher is researching Lake Wobegon1 to see if all the children are really above average, they may use an IQ score with a normal distribution. The researcher is able to find the percentage of people under the age of 19, 29.18% according to the 2000 census.2 Since IQ scores are based on a normal distribution, with 68% of the values for the entire population falling within the normal range, that leave only 16% of scores either above or below the average range. So, even if one could assert that only people over 19 were below average, which would still leave roughly 13% of children in Lake Wobegon falling within the average range of IQ scores.

The oversimplified and fictional example above does make use of the normal curve, but it is not the application commonly applied. Generally, a researcher will determine a level of tolerance for error or confidence they require in their results. If a researcher wants to be 95% sure the answer they conclude is supported, they are willing to accept a 5% probability that the answer is not supported, that the answer will fall in the area outside about 2(1.98) standard deviations. It is a calculated risk. While the researcher does determine what level of probability they wish to call significant, there are three percentages that are used most frequently.

The Levels of Significance most often cited in studies are 0.05, 0.01 and 0.001. Respectively, they can be interpreted as 95% sure the results are due to what is being tested, 99% confident and 99.9% confident. These levels of significance are often called alpha levels, α, the probability of rejecting the null hypothesis when it should have been accepted. Even when a researcher is incredibly diligent in designing and carrying out a study, there is still an element of error associated with sampling and, as such, the results are cited as probabilities. A researcher chooses an alpha level before data collection and analysis, and may report it as a probability, ($p \leq .05$) or may report the data will be analyzed at the $\alpha = .05$ level of significance.

Accepting or Rejecting the Null

Rejecting or Accepting the Null Hypothesis is based not only on the data collected but also on the level of significance at which the data were analyzed. If a researcher is studying the sleeping habits of teenage boys with video game systems as opposed to those teenage boys without game systems, they may set the level of significance at $p \leq .05$ for the null hypothesis that there is no significant difference between the sleeping habits of the two groups. When all the data were analyzed, the researcher determined that teenage boys with video game systems sleep 1.25 hours less per week with a $p = .40$. The researcher is not

---

[1] Lake Wobegon is a fictional location created by Garrison Keillor for his Prairie Home Companion® Radio broadcast from Minnesota Public Radio. It is described by Keillor as the little town where "all the women are strong, all the men are good looking, and all the children are above average."

[2] As Lake Wobegon is fictional, the data presented are not from Lake Wobegon, rather they are from the non-fiction state of Minnesota.

able to reject the null hypothesis because the p=.40 means that there is a 40% chance that the 1.25 hour difference is due to something other than the video game system.

One way a researcher can address this scenario is to modify the null hypothesis, the data collection procedures, experiment design or increase the sample size. By increasing the sample size, the researcher increases the likelihood of a normal distribution and reduces the effect of outliers. In the scenario above, the researcher included a wider age range and included more subjects in their second trial. The researcher kept the .05 alpha level and found that teenage and pre-teen boys slept 1.30 hours less per week, p=.06. This is still not statistically significant, as p=.06 indicates that there is a 6% probability that the difference is not due to the video game system, but the results were more promising than in the earlier, more narrow study. The researcher was very excited by these results and wanted to claim that pre-teen boys who have video systems get less sleep than those who do not. A colleague gently suggested that it was premature to make that claim. Always keep in mind, only the hypothesis being tested can be rejected or accepted.

While the data do appear to indicate that including pre-teen boys in the data yielded significant results, that is not what was tested, the hypothesis included both teenage and pre-teen boys. If the researcher were to change the null hypothesis, they may very well find a significant difference, one with a $p \leq .05$, but that would be a different study.

Exercise 6.

Evaluating Significance.

1. If a study has been conducted and the results are found to have a $p = .033$ level of significance, would that cause the researcher to reject or accept the null If the study were designed to test the $\alpha = .05$ level of significance? What about the $\alpha = .01$ level of significance?

2. How do you think the sample size and protocol affects the level of significance a researcher chooses for their research?

3. Compare the normal curve; Figure 3-2, to a skewed distribution; figure 1-5, why would a researcher hesitate to draw conclusions if the data fall into a skewed distribution?

4. What does a $p = .12$ value represent?

Type I and Type II Error

Type I and Type II Error are results of sampling and can not be fully eliminated. Every inferential statistic has its own sampling distribution, and that distribution has inherent sampling error. A researcher can not know for certain that what they observed/measured was really caused by your manipulation (treatment) or whether it was due to chance alone.

The level of significance is directly connected to sampling error and the sampling distribution. The level of significance was the confidence level at which the hypothesis could be rejected, based on the sampling distribution. A sampling distribution is a theoretical distribution that would occur if all possible samples of the same size were randomly selected for the population of interest, and computing a statistic for each sample. If the statistic calculated for the sample being studied meets the criterion for significance, then the null hypothesis will be rejected. If the alpha level is .05, then there is a 95% level of certainty that the results are due to what the researcher is testing. That unaccounted for 5% is a Type I error. The level of significance is the probability of making a Type I error. In the earlier discussion of choosing lollipop colors, the null hypothesis was that there would be no significant difference in lollipop color preference of 3-year olds. If the data show that the researcher should reject the null hypothesis, that there is a significant difference in color preference, but that was not true, the researcher has made a Type I error. Type I error can be addressed because it is related to sampling.

To reduce Type I error, researchers increase their sample size, or try to make their sampling more representative. If the sample better represents the population to which conclusions will be inferred, then it is less likely findings will be due to chance, and therefore the level of confidence will be higher and the probability of a Type I error will be lower.

The other type of error, Type II error, is more difficult to quantify. Type II error occurs when the researcher fails to reject the null when it was, in fact, false. This type of error is unknown and unknowable. As the level of confidence increases, the chance of making a Type II error increases, even as the chance of making a Type I error decreases. The terminology fail to reject the null is very formal, and is used by convention. Type II error is accepting a false null hypothesis. In the lollipop example, if the researcher found that there was no difference in preference they would accept (fail to reject) the null hypothesis. If there was truly a difference in the color preference of 3-year olds, this would have been an example of Type II error, but the researcher would never know it.

Table 3-1. Summary of Type I and Type II Error

	Null is True.	Null is False.
Null is accepted. (Fail to reject the null.)		Type II Error
Null is rejected.	Type I Error	

Exercise 7.

Types of Error.

1. If a researcher is designing a study to evaluate the effectiveness of a program, why might they choose a .01 level of significance instead of a .05 level? What would that mean in terms of Type I and Type II error?

2. Give an example of a scenario where a researcher would prefer to have a higher Type I error?

3. Why might a researcher accept a higher Type II error in return for a lower Type I error?

Questions for Discussion

1. As a researcher, there are constraints on resources such as time, money, or access to subjects that are beyond the researcher's control. How might these constraints affect the design of a study?

2. Why do researchers use the null form of the hypothesis for statistical analyses?

3. How are the two types of error connected to the normal distribution?

4. Propose a research question and directional hypothesis.

5. What are the null and alternate hypotheses?

6. At what level of significance would you evaluate your null hypothesis?

7. Why did you choose that level of significance?

8. What does that mean in terms of Type I and Type II error?

9. If your data show p=0.032, what can you say about your hypothesis?

10. What does that mean in terms of Type I and Type II error?

Chapter Four:
Choosing a Test

This chapter is designed to help determine the appropriate statistical test to be used in data analysis. After a general introduction, the tests are listed based on criteria specific to a study. Based on the design of the study, and the data to be analyzed the method of analysis is determined (Table 4-1).

Questions to Ask

When a researcher chooses a test they answer the following questions:

* ❋ What is the level of measurement of my independent and dependent variable?
* ❋ How many groups are there?
* ❋ Are the groups dependent or independent of each other?
* ❋ Does the null hypothesis call for a comparison (difference) or a relationship?
* ❋ If the level of measurement is at least interval—are any of the assumptions for using a parametric test violated?
  * o ASSUMPTIONS
    * ▪ Are the data normally distributed?
    * ▪ Are the variances equal?
    * ▪ Is the sample large enough?

These questions will help the researcher choose the appropriate test. Unfortunately, it is possible to apply the wrong test to data and the results will look just as reasonable as if the correct test was chosen. A researcher must be clear on the answers to these questions if they want to find practical and statistical significance with their research.

Table 4-1. Criteria and Methods of Analysis

Level of Measurement	Descriptive		Comparative	Relationship
	Central Tendency	Dispersion		
Nominal	Mode (Mo)	Range (R)	Chi-Square (χ^2)	Phi-Prime (φ') Contingency Coefficient (c)
Ordinal	Median (MD)	Semi-Interquartile (Range) (Q)	Mann Whitney Wilcoxon T	
Interval	Mean (μ), ($\bar{x}$)	Std. Dev. (σ) Variance (σ^2)	T-test independent samples T-test dependent samples ANOVA	Pearson Product Moment coefficient of correlation (R)
Ratio	Mean (μ), ($\bar{x}$)	Std. Dev. (σ) Variance (σ^2)	T-test independent samples T-test dependent samples ANOVA	Pearson Product Moment coefficient of correlation (R)

Once the test has been selected, the researcher must decide whether the analysis will be done by hand or with the aid of a statistical program. If the calculations are to be computed manually, the degrees of freedom must be established. The number of degrees of freedom is defined as the number of values that are free to vary after restriction has been placed on the data. So if a researcher were to have four responses, there would be three degrees of freedom (n-1) because there are three other options when one has been chosen. Many published sampling distributions take the degrees of freedom and the level of significance into account. In general, the lower the degrees of freedom the more difficult the hypothesis will be to reject. If you use computer statistical test programs, the degrees of freedom and the actual alpha level are computed automatically.

Inferential Tests for Nominal Data

One Group Tests for Nominal Data

Binomial Test (Nonparametric Test)

REQUIREMENTS:
- ❋ Nominal Data
- ❋ One-Group
- ❋ Two Categories Only
- ❋ Sample Size Can Be Less Than 5.
- ❋ Independent Observations
- ❋ Simple Random Sample
- ❋ Data In Frequency Form

When the sample increases in size, calculations become cumbersome—so other tests are used. If a researcher wants to calculate this by hand they would need to establish a null hypothesis that states that there is no difference in the probability of one outcome versus another, like the choice of red vs. purple lollipop for one 3-year old; that 50% of the time the choice will be the red lollipop and the other half will be the purple. If each choice has an equal likelihood then the probability that the child will choose red 3 times in a row is ½ x ½ x ½ or (½)3 or .125. If the choice were offered 20 times, the likelihood that the child would always choose red is (½)20 and if it were n times the probability would equal (½)n. If we call the number of trials n, the number of times we have the desired outcome (red) k, and the proportion of times we expect to get red (k) if the null hypothesis is true then we can set up a binomial test. A generalized equation form of the binomial test is:

$$Y = \frac{p^k (1-p)^{(n-k)} n!}{k!(n-k)!}$$

where Y is the probability of having the desired outcome (k) in the number of trials (n). In a scenario where we wanted to evaluate whether there was no significant difference in the number of times a red lollipop was chosen compared to purple lollipop at the 0.05 level of confidence, we would ask a child n times and record the times they choose red. If we asked the child to choose 6 times and out of those 6 times, red was chosen 4 the equation would be:

$$Y = \frac{0.5^4 (1-0.5)^{(6-4)} 6!}{4!(6-4)!}$$

$$Y = \frac{(0.0625)(0.5)^2(6 \cdot 5 \cdot 4 \cdot 3 \cdot 2 \cdot 1)}{(4 \cdot 3 \cdot 2 \cdot 1)(2!)}$$

$$Y = \frac{(0.0625)(.25)(720)}{(24)(2 \cdot 1)}$$

$$Y = \frac{11.25}{48}$$

$$Y = .23475$$

Since 0.23 is not less than .05 we would not be able to reject the null. This example had a very small n, as the number of trials increases, the calculations quickly become overwhelming.

Chi-Square Test for Goodness Of Fit (Nonparametric Test)

REQUIREMENTS
* Nominal Data
* One-Group Test
* One Or More Categories
* Independent Observations
* Adequate Sample Size
* For 2 Categories (Male/Female) Expected Frequencies Must Be 5 Or Larger.
* For More Than 2 Categories, No More Than 20% Of The Categories Should Be Smaller Than 5.
* Simple Random Sample
* Data In Frequency Form
* All Observations Must Be Used
* Two Tail Test Only.

The Chi-square goodness of fit test is used to determine if a significant difference exists between expected frequencies and the observed frequencies in one or more categories. The bigger the value of chi-square, the larger is the difference between the observed and expected frequencies; the better chance for a significant difference to have occurred. This test is used to determine whether data fit an expected pattern or distribution, so it is important that the expected pattern or distribution be quantifiable.

To calculate a chi-square manually, every observed value is subtracted from the expected value. The difference generated is squared and divided by the expected value, and all these numbers are added together. Mathematically this is shown:

$$chi^2 = \sum \frac{(O-E)^2}{E}$$

Generally, samples are large enough that one would have a computer calculate the chi-square, but for example you were playing a game with dice and you wanted to know if the dice were fair, you could calculate a chi-square. You would expect that each die had an equal chance of landing on any of the six sides, 1/6 or .167. That is, if one die was rolled one hundred times, it would be expected to land on a ⊡ 16.7% of the time. If the hypothesis were that the die was fair, that is there was no significant difference between this die and a fair die and out of 600 throws of the die, it would land on ⊡ 100 times. Additionally it would land on ⠒ and the other sides 100 times. When the die in question was rolled 100 times, it had the following results:

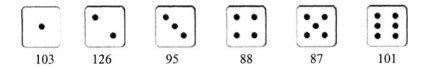

| 103 | 126 | 95 | 88 | 87 | 101 |

Using the results above and the chi-square equation the following chi-square statistic can be calculated:

$$chi^2 = \frac{(103-100)^2}{100} + \frac{(126-100)^2}{100} + \frac{(95-100)^2}{100} + \frac{(88-100)^2}{100} + \frac{(87-100)^2}{100} + \frac{(101-100)^2}{100}$$

$$chi^2 = \frac{9}{100} + \frac{676}{100} + \frac{25}{100} + \frac{144}{100} + \frac{169}{100} + \frac{1}{100}$$

$$chi^2 = 10.24$$

Once the chi-square statistic is calculated, the critical value for .05 level of significance found in a published table and compared to the statistic 10.24. The statistic is lower than the published critical value, and so there is a 95% chance that the results do not fall outside the normal range. Based on this the null can not be rejected, the die is fair.

Alternately, the data could be entered into a statistical program like SPSS. When SPSS analyzed the same data it calculated the Chi-square test statistic and an actual value for the asymmetrical significance (Table 4-2). The significance value calculated by SPSS is 0.069, and being larger than the 0.05 level of significance, we fail to reject the null. Note that both the manually calculated and computer generated chi square statistics yield the same result.

Table 4-2 Chi-Square Test Statistics generated by SPSS

	Die Value
Chi-Square(a)	10.240
df	5
Asymp. Sig.	.069

a   0 cells (.0%) have expected frequencies less than 5. The minimum expected cell frequency is 100.0.

Table 4-3 Observed Frequency of Values on Die

	Observed N	Expected N	Residual
1.00	103	100.0	3.0
2.00	126	100.0	26.0
3.00	95	100.0	-5.0
4.00	88	100.0	-12.0
5.00	87	100.0	-13.0
6.00	101	100.0	1.0
Total	600		

Two Groups Tests for Nominal Data

Fisher's Exact Test (Nonparametric)

REQUIREMENTS:
* Nominal Data
* Two Groups
* One-tail or Two-tail

The Fisher's exact test is best calculated by computer, as it involves a large volume of calculations. The calculations are not difficult to perform, but the sheer volume of calculations makes it well suited to computer software. For the curious, the formula for the Fisher's Exact test is solved with a matrix, if we label the rows R and the columns C for an m x n matrix with entries up to x=i and y=j, the probability is calculated:

$$P_{cutoff} = \frac{(R_1!R_2!\cdots R_m!)(C_1!C_2!\cdots C_n!)}{N!\prod_{ij} a_{ij}!}$$

The P cutoff value can be compared to the level of significance to determine whether the hypothesis can be rejected.

Two or More Groups Tests for Nominal Data

Chi-Square for Independent Groups (Nonparametric)

REQUIREMENTS:
* ❋ Nominal Data
* ❋ Two Or More Groups
* ❋ Independent Groups
* ❋ Adequate Sample Size.
* ❋ Expected Frequency of 5 or More
* ❋ Two Tailed Test Only

Chi-square can be used to determine if 2 or more groups differ significantly on any given characteristic. The chi-square is more likely to show significance if the sample is large, the relationship is strong, or the actual data are large in value. The chi-square calculations are the same as for the chi-square goodness of fit, with the addition of the calculation of the degrees of freedom. For the chi-square the degrees of freedom value is the product of the number of levels of the first variable (C) minus one multiplied by the number of levels of the second variable (R) minus one.

$$df = (C-1)(R-1)$$

If the data are fewer than five in frequency, then the Fischer Exact test should be used.

More Than Two Groups for Nominal Data

Cochran Q Test (Nonparametric)

REQUIREMENTS
* Nominal Data
* Three Or More Groups
* Dependent Groups
* Dichotomous Variables Only (0=failure, 1=success)
* Data In Frequency Form
* Two Tail Test Only

The Cochran Q test is used to look for differences in more than two sets of dichotomous data. The groups of data should be dependent; this may look like several different individuals' results on the same condition, or different conditions on the same individuals. However it is applied, the data must be dichotomous, or manipulated to be dichotomous and able to be tabulated into frequencies.

The manual computation for the Cochran Q uses the generalized formula:

$$Q = \frac{SS_A}{MS_{A/S}}$$

This is read as the sum of squares for factor A is divided by the mean squared A within S. While this looks and sounds complicated, the computation behind it is not. To calculate the sum of squares is just the square of the difference between the individual data point and the average data point.

$$SS = \sum_{i=1}^{n} (X_i - \overline{X})^2$$

The mean square is the average variance of the scores, so each score is subtracted from the mean (average) score and the difference squared. All these numbers are added up and then divided by the total number of scores to calculate the average.

$$MS = \frac{SS}{df}$$

The degrees of freedom (df) for within groups is the difference between the number of subjects or observations and the number of groups. If N is the number of subjects, and K is the number of groups,

$$df = N - K.$$

So, while each part of the calculation is not difficult, the use of software to calculate the Q value and compare it to a critical value is often preferred.

Inferential Tests for Ordinal Data

One Group Test for Ordinal Data

Kolmogorov Smirnov Test (Nonparametric)

REQUIREMENTS
* Ordinal Data
* One Group
* Simple Random Sample
* Continuous Distributions

This test is used to determine if a distribution of actual observations are significantly different from a theoretical distribution like the Chi-square. The difference between the two is that the Chi-square goodness of fit tests the overall closeness of the values to the expected value and the one-sample Kolmogorov-Smirnov test can compare individual values of the data set. This makes it a more powerful test when the assumptions of the test are met.

The Kolmogorov-Smirnov test can be applied to any continuous distribution as it is comparing the curve of the expected to the curve of the observed and testing the differences in the curves at any given point. Mathematically, the test can be written:

$$D = \max_{1 < i < N} \left(F(Y_i) - \frac{i-1}{N}, \frac{i}{N} - F(Y_i) \right)$$

The test statistic D can be compared to a value in a published table to determine significance. In the above equation, F represents the distribution being tested, N is the number of samples and the two fractions address the difference from the expected curve and the observed curve.

Generally, this test is performed by software, either a program specifically designed to analyze statistics, or a web-based calculator. These calculators will take into account that there are several versions of the

Kolmogorov-Smirnov available and the table of critical values must have been calculated using the same equation. There are slight variations in critical values depending on the published source used.

Two Group Tests for Ordinal Data

Mann-Whitney Test (Nonparametric)

REQUIREMENTS
* ❋ Ordinal Data
* ❋ Two Groups
* ❋ Independent Groups
* ❋ Ranked Data
* ❋ Simple Random Samples
* ❋ May Have Unequal Sample Sizes

The Mann-Whitney Test, sometimes referred to as the Mann-Whitney U is used to determine if a difference exists between the rankings of two independent groups. It is very useful if the sample is small or the assumption that the data fit a normal curve can not be satisfied.

If computer software, or Internet-based computational software is not to be used, the researcher must first rank the data from lowest to highest, including ties if the data require. The data must be separated into the two groups, after the ranking is completed. Once the two samples (n1 and n2) are set and the ranks (Ri) are established they can be used in the following formula to calculate U:

$$U = n_1 n_2 + \frac{n_2(n_2+1)}{2} - \sum_{i-n_i+1}^{n_2} R_i$$

While the equation looks intimidating, it is quite easy to calculate manually. If we wanted to determine who was better at staring, boys or girls, we could set up an experiment where we had 5 boys and 5 girls, their scores in seconds are listed in the following table.

Table 4-4 Boys and Girls Times Staring at a Point (seconds)

Girls Time	Rank	Rank	Boys Time
		1	16
		2	24
		3.5	33
33	3.5		
59	5		
64	6		
		7	65
		8	74
77	9		
146	10		
	R1=33.5	R2=21.5	

$$U_1 = n_1 n_2 + \frac{n_2(n_2+1)}{2} - \sum_{i-n_i+1}^{n_2} R_i$$

$$U_1 = 5 \cdot 5 + \frac{5(6)}{2} - 33.5$$

$$= 25 + 15 - 33.5$$

$$= 6.5$$

$$U_2 = n_1 n_2 + \frac{n_2(n_2+1)}{2} - \sum_{i-n_i+1}^{n_2} R_i$$

$$U_2 = 5 \cdot 5 + \frac{5(6)}{2} - 21.5$$

$$= 25 + 15 - 21.5$$

$$= 18.5$$

Once the values for U have been calculated they can be compared to a value in a published table. For a sample of 5, the critical value is 2. If the calculated U is lower than the Ucrit from the published table, then the null hypothesis that there is no difference can be rejected. In this case, the null can not be rejected because neither U value is lower than the Ucrit of 2.

Wilcoxon-Ranks Test (Nonparametric)

REQUIREMENTS
  ✳ Ordinal Data
  ✳ Two Groups
  ✳ Dependent Groups
  ✳ Pairs of data are independent from other pairs of data
  ✳ Ranked Data
  ✳ Dependent Variable Continuous

The Wilcoxon-ranks test is used to compare the distributions of ranks of two dependent groups. This test is similar to the Mann-Whitney test in that all the data are ranked, but there are two large differences. The first is that the ranks are based on the differences in the scores, and the second is that the positive/negative relationship is retained. To calculate the test statistic, the positive ranks are added.

$$W = \sum_{i=1}^{n'} R_i^{(+)}$$

This will provide a value that can be compared to a one-tailed critical value from a published table. If there are more than 20 in the sample (n'), a Z approximation formula is used. The large sample (>20) approximation formula is:

$$Z = \frac{W - \mu_W}{\sigma_W}$$

The test statistic Z is used to determine whether the null may be rejected if the sample is large, or the comparison of the test statistic W to the Wcrit from a table is used for the determination. Computer software will calculate the probability automatically, and that can be compared to the level of significance regardless of the sample size.

Three or More Groups Tests for Ordinal Data

Kruskal-Wallis Test (Nonparametric)

REQUIREMENTS
- ❋ Ordinal Data
- ❋ Three Or More Groups
- ❋ Independent Groups
- ❋ Simple Random Sample

The Kruskal-Wallis test is an extension of the Mann-Whitney test and uses the pooled ranks from more than 2 groups. It is the nonparametric alternative to the one-way analysis of variance. If Ri is the sum of all the ranks, Ni the number of data points from a sample and N the number of all the data points from all samples combined, the Kruskal-Wallis test statistic can be calculated using the formula:

$$H = \frac{12}{N(N+1)} \sum \frac{R_1^2}{N_1} - 3(N+1)$$

If the H calculated is larger than the critical value listed in a published table, the null would be rejected. There is a nuance that is not obvious, ties affect the H statistic. There are correction factors that can be applied to account for the ties, and they should be employed if there are many ties and the H value is close to the critical value. Again, if a statistical program is utilized, the probability will be calculated automatically. If the tied data statistic is to be calculated manually using the formula:

$$H = \frac{12}{N(N+1)} \sum_{j=1}^{k} n_j \left(\overline{R}_j - \frac{N+1}{2} \right)^2$$

Friedman Test (Nonparametric)

REQUIREMENTS
- ❋ Ordinal Data
- ❋ Three Or More Groups

   ❋   Dependent Groups
   ❋   Sample Selected Randomly From Dependent Groups
   ❋   Data are continuous

The Friedman's test is the nonparametric alternative to the repeated measures analysis of variance, and is used to determine if a significant difference exists among three or more dependent groups. The test is similar to the chi-square, determining whether (k) samples come from the same population. It does this by asserting that if groups do not vary on the tested variable, then the average ranks of the subjects measured by the tested variable will not differ between groups.

A use of the Friedman test is inter-rater reliability, where one is looking to see if multiple raters differ when looking at a series of items. If the test is calculated manually, the equation is similar to the chi-square and the Kruskal-Wallis, and it is:

$$\chi^2 = \frac{12}{nk(k+1)} \sum (T_g)^2 - 3n(k+1)$$

where T = the sum of all the ranks $\left(\frac{nk(k+1)}{2}\right)$, n = the number of subjects and k = the measures per subject. There are several web-based programs that will perform all the calculations, even the ranking of raw data; as will other software programs. Additionally, these programs will compute the probability that differences are due to chance alone, instead of using published tables to compare the calculated test statistic with a critical value.

Inferential Tests for Interval/Ratio Data

One Group Tests for Interval/Ratio Data

T Test (Parametric)

REQUIREMENTS
   ❋   At Least Interval Data
   ❋   Random Sample
   ❋   Sample Drawn From A Normally Distributed Population

The first of three types of t-test is the one-sample t-test. It is used with one group samples where the population has a normal distribution, and the population mean is known. If the t statistic is to be calculated manually, the equation for "t" may be used:

$$t = \frac{x - \mu}{s / \sqrt{n}}$$ where df = n-1.

The result of this calculation is compared to values found in a published table. This allows the researcher to take a sample from a population, compute a mean($\square$) and compare it to the assumed mean of the population (μ). If a computer program is used, it will likely calculate the p-value. The t-test can be used as a one-tailed or two-tailed test depending on whether a directional or non-directional hypothesis is being tested.

Two Group Tests for Interval/Ratio Data

T-Test for Independent Means (Parametric)

REQUIREMENTS
* At Least Interval Data
* Independent Groups
* Normal Distribution Of Population
* Variances Are Equal
* Random Samples

This form of the t-test is used to determine if a significant difference exists between the means of two independent groups. This is the parametric alternate to the Mann-Whitney test. If a researcher does not choose to use a computer to perform the calculations the following formula can be used:

$$t_{\overline{x_1} - \overline{x_2}} = \frac{\overline{X}_1 - \overline{X}_2}{\sqrt{\left[\frac{(N_1 - 1)s_1^2 + (N_2 - 1)s_2^2}{N_1 + N_2 - 2}\right]\left(\frac{1}{N_1} + \frac{1}{N_2}\right)}}$$

The first term in the square root, the bracketed term, is known as the common variance. The common variance is shared between the samples because it is due to the variance of the population from which both were drawn.

Both one-tailed and two-tailed tests are possible, depending on how the hypothesis has been written. Depending on the test, one-tailed or two, there is a different critical value to determine whether there is a significant difference between the means.

Paired T-Test (Parametric)

REQUIREMENTS
* At Least Interval Data
* Dependent Groups
* Normal Distribution Of Population
* Equal Variances
* Random Samples

The paired sample t-test is used to determine if a significant difference exists between the means of two dependent groups. Examples of dependent groups would be pre and post tests, matched pairs, or case control studies. Interestingly, the paired sample t-test is not computed the same way as the independent sample test. If one is manually computing the paired samples t-test the following equation is used:

$$t = (\overline{X} - \overline{Y}) \sqrt{\frac{n(n-1)}{\sum_{i=1}^{n}(\hat{X}_i - \hat{Y}_i)^2}}$$

with df = n-1

where Xi and Yi are two paired sets of n values. Once the t value has been calculated it is compared with a value from a published table based on the degrees of freedom. This tcrit is compared to the calculated value. If the calculated t value (tcomp) is positive, then the null hypothesis is rejected when tcomp $\geq$ tcrit, one tail, and if the calculated value is negative, then the hypothesis is rejected when tcomp $\leq$ -tcrit, one tail.

More Than 2 Groups Tests for Interval/Ratio Data

One-Way Analysis of Variance (Parametric)

REQUIREMENTS
* Normally Distributed Population
* Equal Variances
* Three Or More Independent Groups
* Random Sample
* At Least Interval Data

The one-way analysis of variance, ANOVA, is used to determine if a significant difference exists among the means of three or more independent groups and one independent variable. ANOVA determines if the variance among the means is a function of chance alone by comparing the mean values of each group with the overall mean of the entire data set. If the means for each group are similar, they will be similar to the overall mean, and conversely, if they are not similar, then the group means will be different from the overall mean. The ANOVA is an extension of the t-test.

ANOVA is the parametric equivalent to the non-parametric Kruskal-Wallis test. Unlike the Kruskal-Wallis, one-way ANOVA does not depend on rankings, but uses the raw data. Similar to its non-parametric counterpart, the computations are tedious for the ANOVA. If there are only three groups P, Q, and R, there are three test statistics required: 1) comparing P and Q, 2) comparing Q and R, and 3) comparing P and R. This number of combinations grows exponentially as the number of groups increases.

Using a computer program like SPSS, an ANOVA output shows the sum of squares between and within groups, mean square values between and within groups, the F statistic, and the significance value.

Table 4-5 SPSS ANOVA Output for Four Groups

	Sum of Squares	df	Mean Square	F	Sig.
Between Groups	210279.787	3	70093.262	58.960***	.000
Within Groups	2292044.600	1928	1188.820		
Total	2502324.387	1931			

The third column in the ANOVA output (Table 4-5) contained the degrees of freedom between groups (# of groups – 1), degrees of freedom within groups (n - # of groups), and total degrees of freedom (n – 1). In this case the dfbetween was 3 because there were 4 groups; dfwithin was 1928, because there were 1932 subjects and 4 groups and dftotal was 1931.

The fourth column presented the Mean Square (MS) for between groups (70,000) and for within groups (1200). The MSbetween was calculated by dividing the SSbetween (210,000) by the dfbetween (3). The MSwithin was calculated in the same way, SSwithin (2,300,00) ÷ dfwithin (1928).

The fifth and sixth columns of Table 4-5 exhibited the final F statistic and its level of significance. The F statistic, or F ratio was determined by dividing the MSbetween by the MSwithin. The F statistic determined that there was a significant difference between at least two of the groups. In this case, the F is 59, which was significant at the $p \leq .001$ alpha level. The significance level generated by SPSS was 0.000, which is less than the .001 alpha level. This means that there is a less than 1 in a 1000 chance that the differences in the means was due to chance alone, but does not specify for which groups the differences exist.

To do these manually, a series of formulae would be used. The between group sum of squares is calculated with:

$$SS_b = \sum_g \left[\frac{(\sum X_g)^2}{N_g} \right] - \frac{(\sum X)^2}{N}$$

To calculate the within group sum of squares, use:

$$SS_w = \sum_g \left[\sum X_g^2 - \frac{(\sum X_g)^2}{N_g} \right]$$

And the total sum of squares formula:

$$SS_{tot} = \sum X^2 - \frac{(\sum X)^2}{N}$$

Also required are the between groups means square:

$$MS_b = \frac{SS_b}{df_b} \text{, where df} = \text{k-1}$$

Within group mean square formula:

$$MS_w = \frac{SS_w}{df_w} \text{, where df} = \text{n-k}$$

And, the F ratio.

$$F = \frac{MS_b}{MS_w}$$

The calculated F ratio can be compared to critical values and using the degrees of freedom associated with the numerator (MS_b) and the denominator

(MS_w) of the F ratio. If the calculated F ratio value is higher than the critical value of F, the null hypothesis is rejected.

The ANOVA tests the significance of the difference among the means simultaneously, it does not differentiate between the groups, or identify the nature of the comparison. To determine which of the groups are significantly different from each other, post hoc analyses are used.

Contrast Tests for ANOVA

The ANOVA does not tell where a difference exists among groups, only that it does exist. Contrast tests are used if a significant difference is found by the use of ANOVA to determine which groups are significantly different from each other, and the nature of those differences.

Three common contrast tests are the Fisher Least Significant Difference (LSD), the Scheffe Test and the Tukey Honestly Significant Difference (HSD) (Figure 4-1). There are various other tests available to researchers, but these three are quite common.

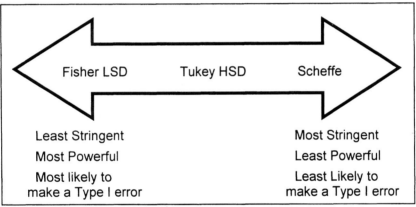

Figure 4-1 A comparison of post hoc tests.

If a researcher finds a significant F ratio, then they may employ a post hoc test to determine where the difference lies. In order to determine which groups have significant differences manually, the researcher must create a table of differences of the means of the groups. The groups should be listed in the table from lowest (1) to highest (k) the differences in the means are then listed in the table (Figure 4-2). The value in the table of differences will serve as the comparison once the critical difference is calculated. If the value in the table is greater than or equal to the calculated critical difference then the two groups are significantly different. To calculate the critical difference a researcher would use one of the following formulae.

Group	1	2	3	...k
1	-	$\bar{X}_1 - \bar{X}_2$	$\bar{X}_2 - \bar{X}_3$	$\bar{X}_{...} - \bar{X}_k$
2		-	$\bar{X}_2 - \bar{X}_3$	$\bar{X}_{...} - \bar{X}_k$
3			-	$\bar{X}_{...} - \bar{X}_k$
...k				-

Figure 4-2 Table of differences

The Fisher LSD:

$$CD_{LSD} = t_{crit} \sqrt{2 \left(\frac{MS_{S/A}}{n} \right)}$$

Tukey HSD:

$$CD_{Tukey} = q \sqrt{\frac{MS_{S/A}}{n}}$$

Scheffe Test:

$$CD_{Scheffe} = q \sqrt{\frac{MS_{S/A}}{n}} \text{ where } q = \sqrt{2(a-1)F_{(a-1df_{S/A})}}$$

For both the Fisher LSD and the Tukey HSD the same critical difference (CD) can be used for each cell of the table of differences. For the Scheffe test, each cell has a different CD. The value for "A" in the equation represents the number of levels of the independent variable tested. With the availability of computer programs to calculate statistical tests, the researcher does not, in general, compute these values manually. The correct test is selected based on the researcher's requirements and the nature of the data and the computer program is charged with the task of computation.

Repeated Measures ANOVA

REQUIREMENTS
* Normally Distributed Population
* Equal Variances
* Three Or More Dependent Groups
* Random Sample
* At Least Interval Data

The repeated measures analysis of variance and the multivariate analysis of variance (MANOVA) expand the applications of the one-way analysis of variance (ANOVA). Like the way the Kolmogorov-Smirnov and the Mann-Whitney build on the Chi-square to expand the application of the test, the repeated measures ANOVA and MANOVA expand the used of the ANOVA.

The repeated measures ANOVA is similar to the paired t-test, in that the groups are dependent. This test increases the likelihood of finding a significant difference because each subject is its own control, minimizing the variance due to sampling error. If a researcher wanted to compute the sum of squares SS_{subj} manually, the formula

$$SS_{subj} = \sum_{s} \left[\frac{(\sum X_m)^2}{K} \right] - \frac{(\sum X)^2}{N}$$

would be employed. As in earlier formulae, K represents the number of groups of scores, X_m is the mean for each subject, and Σ is the sum of those means. The symbol Σ with the subscript s is the sum across all subjects, and N is the number of subjects. Notice how similar this formula is to the ANOVA formula to determine the between group sum of squares. The mean squares is found the same way it is for the ANOVA, divide the sum of squares by the degrees of freedom.

The repeated measures ANOVA is used when a researcher is conducting a longitudinal study. If a researcher wanted to test the effectiveness of a writing program and tested students writing before, during, at the conclusion of and after the completion of the program, a repeated measures ANOVA would be the appropriate test. Looking back, if the parametric assumptions can not be met, the Friedman test is the nonparametric equivalent for the repeated measures ANOVA. If the researcher wanted to compare the boys and girls performance during the course of the writing program, the repeated measures ANOVA should not be used, as gender is a separate independent variable. Gender is not a different condition rather it is a different quality entirely. In this case, with multiple independent variables, a MANOVA should be utilized.

There are a few reasons that a researcher may choose to run a MANOVA test instead of several one-way ANOVA tests. Because the MANOVA can compare several dependent and independent variables in the same experiment, the researcher has a greater chance of determining which factors are connected with a significant difference. The MANOVA reduces type I error as compared to running several one-way ANOVAs and may show the researcher differences that are statistically significant that may have not been revealed with separate ANOVA tests.

While these are compelling reasons to employ a MANOVA, a researcher may hesitate because of some of the MANOVA's drawbacks. Both the independent and dependent variables should be clearly independent of each other to reduce confusion when evaluating which independent variable is affecting each dependent variable. Additionally, for every dependent variable added to the MANOVA a degree of freedom is sacrificed. The MANOVA does offer more statistical power, but if a researcher adds too many dependent variables, that additional power may be lost in the fewer degrees of freedom.

The manual computation is complex. Actually, that is an enormous understatement. Like the Fisher's exact test, the MANOVA uses a matrix to solve for the possible combinations of factors, but unlike the Fisher's exact test, the calculations in the matrix are similar to the ANOVA. The calculations still involve the sum of squares between and within groups, but then the sum of squares between groups is broken down into the variance for each independent variable and the interactions between those independent variables. The general equation is:

$$n_{km}\sum_{k}\sum_{m}(DT_{km}-GM_{(DT)})^2 = n_k\sum_{k}\left(D_k-GM_{(D)}\right)^2 + n_m\sum_{m}\left(T_m-GM_{(T)}\right)^2 +$$

$$\left[n_{km}\sum_{k}\sum_{m}\left(DT_{km}-GM_{(DT)}\right)^2 - n_k\sum_{k}\left(D_k-GM_{(D)}\right)^2 - n_m\sum_{m}\left(T_m-GM_{(T)}\right)^2\right]$$

And the full factorial design for setting up the matrix is:

$$\sum_i \sum_k \sum_m (Y_{ikm} - GM_{(ikm)})^2 = n_k \sum_k (D_k - GM_{(D)})^2 + n_m \sum_m (T_m - GM_{(T)})^2 +$$

$$\left[n_{km} \sum_k \sum_m (DT_{km} - GM_{(DT)})^2 - n_k \sum_k (D_k - GM_{(D)})^2 - n_m \sum_m (T_m - GM_{(T)})^2 \right]$$

$$+ \sum_i \sum_k \sum_m (Y_{ikm} - DT_{km})^2$$

The sum of squares equation is then:

$$\sum_i \sum_k \sum_m (Y_{ikm} - GM)(Y_{ikm} - GM)' = n_k \sum_k (D_k - GM)(D_k - GM)'$$

$$+ n_m \sum_m (T_m - GM)(T_m - GM)' + [n_{km} \sum_{km} (DT_{km} - GM)(DT_{km} - GM)'$$

$$- n_k \sum_k (D_k - GM)(D_k - GM)' - n_m \sum_m (T_m - GM)(T_m - GM)']$$

$$+ \sum_i \sum_k \sum_m (Y_{ikm} - DT_{km})(Y_{ikm} - DT_{km})'$$

Which permits the researcher to calculate the test statistic called Wilk's Lambda according to the equation:

$$\Lambda = \frac{|S_{error}|}{|S_{effect} + S_{error}|}$$

or the amount of overlap between the studied independent variable and the dependent variable. From the Wilk's Lambda, the F can be calculated,

$$F(df_1, df_2) = \left(\frac{1-y}{y} \right) \left(\frac{df_2}{df_1} \right)$$

$$where \ y = \Lambda^{1/s}, \ s = \sqrt{\frac{p^2(df_{effect})^2 - 4}{p^2 + (df_{effect})^2 - 5}},$$

$$p = number \ of \ DVs, \ df_1 = p(df_{effect})$$

$$df_2 = s \left[(df_{error}) - \frac{p - df_{effect} + 1}{2} \right] - \left[\frac{p(df_{effect}) - 2}{2} \right]$$

Due to the complex nature of manually computing the F score for the MANOVA, statistical programs like SPSS and Excel are often used. These programs perform all the calculations and provide the researcher with a calculated significance to compare with the level of confidence established as the cutoff.

There are even more complicated tests to analyze covariance but they will not be discussed here. They rely on the underpinnings of the ANOVA the way the repeated measure ANOVA and MANOVA do.

Correlations

Correlation techniques if not tested for significance but used to determine the magnitude and direction of the relationship between variables is a descriptive measure. Each level of measurement has certain appropriate correlational techniques which are used. When correlation coefficients are tested for significance, they relate to testing a hypothesis of association and at that point, are considered to be an inferential statistic (Table 4-6).

Table 4-6 Advantages and Disadvantages of Research Types

Research Type	Advantages	Disadvantages
Correlational Design	Allows study of variables as they are Many variables can be studied at once Can be relatively easy to do	Must guard against mistaken direction of causality
Correlational designs with control variables	Same as above, plus opportunity to rule out alternative explanations for findings	Same as above, but some alternative explanations can be ruled out with control variables
Survey research	Allows study of many variables Can be relatively easy to do	Same as above; also must use sampling methods to avoid bias
Assessment research	Allows study of student test performance In this age of accountability, data are readily available and important	Same as survey research; sampling must avoid bias

Table 4-7 Quick Reference Table

Level Of Data	Desc. Stats	Features	Examples
Nominal	Frequencies Percentage Mode Phi-Coeff Cramers-V C-Conting	1. Categories	Gender Ed Deg.
Ordinal	Frequencies Percentage Ranking Mode Median Semi-Quartile Deviation Spearman Rho Kendall Tau	1. Categories 2. Ranks	Beauty Contest
Interval	Frequencies Percentage Ranking Mode Median Mean St. Deviation St. Error Variance	1. Categories 2. Ranks 3. Equal Units 4. Arbitrary Zero	Test Scores
Ratio	Frequencies Percentage Ranking Mode Median Mean St. Dev. St. Error Variance	1. Categories 2. Ranks 3. Equal Units 4. Absolute Zero	Wgt/Ht Cbc

Statistical techniques classified according to type, number, and measurement scale of variables

		Dependent Variables					
		One			**Two or More**		
		Nominal	Ordinal	Interval	Nominal	Ordinal	Interval
One — Nominal		Chi Square Test for Independence Contingence Coefficient Cochran Q Test	Sign Test, Median Test, Mann-Whitney Test, Kruskal-Wallis One-Way Analysis of Variance	Analysis of Variance Analysis of Covariance			Multiple Discriminant Analysis
Ordinal			Spearman's Rank Correlation Kendall's Rank Correlation	Analysis of Variance Analysis of Covariance			
Interval		Analysis of Variance Analysis of Covariance		Regression Analysis (Multiple Coefficient Correlation)	Analysis of Variance Analysis of Covariance		Multiple Regression Analysis
Two or More — Nominal			Friedman Two-Way Analysis of Variance	Analysis of Variance Analysis of Covariance Factoral Design			Analysis of Variance Analysis of Covariance
Ordinal							
Interval		Multiple Discriminant Analysis	Multiple Regression Analysis		Multiple Discriminant Analysis		Canonical Correlation

Independent Variables

Figure 4-3 Classification of Statistical Techniques

Appendix A: Summary
(For the Confused and/or Paranoid)

Part One - Introduction

These notes are intended to help you understand the relationship(s) between selected research variables (dependent and independent), hypothesis testing, levels of measurement, and appropriate statistical tests.

Levels of Significance:

Levels of Probability are the same as Levels of Significance:
P. < 0.05 = 5 out of 100 by chance alone
P. < 0.01 = 1 out of 100 by chance alone
P. < 0.001 = 1 out of 1000 by chance alone

Type I error: reject a true hypothesis

Type II error: accept a false hypothesis

Note: when you lower the level of probability (significance) and Type I error, you increase the chance of a Type II error.

Levels of Measurement:

Nominal
Ordinal
Interval
Ratio

Remember: Your Levels of Measurement are determined by the nature of the data supplied by the tests or instruments you employ to analyze the relationships between your research variables.

Hypothetical Topic:

"University Trustee Decision Making Style – Impact upon Presidential Job Satisfaction"

       Dependent Variable = Presidential Job Satisfaction
       Independent Variable = U. T. Decision Making Style

Step One: Select an instrument (MSQ) to measure the Dependent Variable. Select an instrument (VROOM) to measure the Independent Variable.

Step Two: Now, suppose the test for the D.V. gives us data at the Interval Level of Measurement and the test used for the I.V. gives us data at the Nominal or Ordinal Level of Measurement – what statistical test would you employ to examine these relationships? As presented in Figure 4-3, the test employed would be: Analysis of Variance (ANOVA)

Step Three: Select your level of probability to analyze the data.

Hypothetical Topic:

"The Relationships Among Principal Role Conflict, Role Ambiguity, Principal Effectiveness, and Teacher Morale"

       Dependent Variable = Teacher Morale
       Independent Variable = Principal Conflict, Ambiguity, & Effectiveness

Step One: Select an instrument (PTO) to measure the Dependent Variable. Select an instrument to measure the Independent Variable.

Step Two: If the test for the D.V. gives us data at the Ordinal Level of Measurement and the test used for the I.V. gives us data at the Nominal Level of Measurement – what statistical test would you employ to examine these relationships? As presented in Figure 4-3, the test employed would be: The Friedman Analysis

Step Three: Select your level of probability to analyze the data.

Part Two – Some Nonparametric Associations

When you have (1) Independent Variable at the Nominal Level of Measurement, and (1) Dependent Variable at the Ordinal Level of Measurement:

Mann-Whitney U Test
Kruskal-Wallis H Test

When you have (1) Independent Variable and (1) Dependent Variable and they are both at the Nominal Level of Measurement:

Chi-Square

When you have (2 or more) Independent Variables at the Nominal Level of Measurement and (1) Dependent Variable at the Ordinal Level of Measurement:

Friedmann Test

Part Three – Some Parametric Associations

Use One-way Analysis of Variance (ANOVA), when the Dependent Variable (1) is at the Interval Level of Measurement and the Independent Variable (1) is at the Ordinal or Nominal Level of Measurement.

Use Spearmann Rank – Order Correlation, when both your Dependent (1) and Independent (1) Variables are at the Ordinal Level of Measurement.

Use Regression Analysis (Multiple Coefficient Correlation), when both your Dependent (1) and Independent (1) Variables are at the Interval Level of Measurement.

Use Multiple Regression Analysis, when you have one Dependent Variable at the Ordinal Level of Measurement and two or more Independent Variables at the Interval Level of Measurement.

Glossary

Alpha – The probability of a type one error. The alpha level is determined before the data are analyzed and it is used to determine whether statistical significance exists. The higher the alpha level the less stringent the qualification for statistical significance, but the greater the chance of a type one error.

Alternate Hypothesis – A second directional hypothesis that proposes the opposite scenario of the first directional hypothesis.

Analysis of Variance – A parametric statistical test used when the dependent variable is at the interval level of measurement. It is the test used to determine whether there is a significant difference between groups.

Assessment Research – The process of evaluating through the use of an assessment. This assessment may take several forms, but the process of using an assessment to evaluate a hypothesis is assessment research.

Beta – The probability of a type two error. This is unknown and unknowable. As the alpha level decreases, the beta level increases.

Bias – A bias exists when the sample tested does not accurately represent the population from which the sample was drawn.

Biased Sample – A sample that does not accurately represent the population.

Bimodal Distribution – A frequency distribution with two peaks. The two peaks may be different heights.

Binomial Test – A nonparametric test for one group with two categories of data in frequency form.

Box and Whisker Plot – A graphic representation of a distribution where the quartiles are marked along a line. The middle two quartiles are shown with a box and the outside quartiles are shown with whiskers.

Categorical Data – This is another name for nominal data. It is the weakest level of measurement, only providing numerical labels for identifying data.

Census – The method of sampling where every member of the population is surveyed.

Chi-Square Goodness of Fit Test – A nonparametric test to determine if a sample's frequencies are significantly different from expected frequencies.

Chi-Square – A nonparametric test that compares a test statistic to the chi-square distribution.

Chi-Square Distribution – A skewed distribution that depends on the degrees of freedom.

Cluster Random Sampling – The probability technique used when a researcher can not design a stratified sample.

Cochran Q Test – A nonparametric, two-tailed test for dichotomous variables with three or more groups.

Confidence Level – The confidence level is the same as the level of significance. If the confidence level is 0.05 then the resulting data must demonstrate that there is at maximum a 5% chance that the conclusions drawn were due to chance, not due to the variable being tested.

Confounding Variable – A confounding variable is anything not being tested that may affect the results. Confounding variables may be controllable or beyond the control of the researcher, but the researcher should discuss possible impacts of confounding variables.

Continuous Data – Data, when graphed, forms a continuous line. Measurements over time would be an example of continuous data. A test for whether data are discrete or continuous is to look at the scale and ask oneself if there is anything halfway between the values on the scale. Height is a continuous variable, there is a measure in between every other value on the scale.

Convenience Sampling – The least expensive form of sampling. It is subject to larger sampling errors. The researcher uses whatever subjects are readily available.

Correlation Coefficient – A correlational coefficient ranges from -1 to 0 to +1. The closer the coefficient is to zero the less of a correlation between the factor being evaluated and the result. As the result approaches 1 or -1, the relationship between variables is stronger. The relationship can either be positive or negative depending on the sign of the coefficient. Generally, a strong correlation is one with a coefficient above 0.8 or below -0.8.

Correlational Design – These studies look for relationships between independent variables and a dependent variable. The data are analyzed to determine a correlation coefficient that will describe the nature of the relationship between the variables.

Criterion Variable – The variable that is being measured in a non-experimental study.

Critical Value – The value at which the relationship or difference is statistically significant. This value changes based on the level of significance chosen before the data were collected.

Dependent Sample/Group – The members of the sample or group interact in some way. They may be the same individuals at different times, pre/post or longitudinal, or they may be related in a way that affects the data collected.

Descriptive Statistics – These numbers give a picture of the data. The mean, median, mode, standard deviation, and range are all descriptive statistics.

Directional Hypothesis – A directional hypothesis asserts the direction of a difference. It predicts the nature of an outcome.

Discrete Data – Discrete data are not continuous, they are data where there are gaps in the values, and can not be graphed with a continuous line. A test for whether data are discrete or continuous is to look at the scale and ask oneself if there is anything halfway between the values on the scale. If one was looking at the colors of candy covered chocolates, there are green and yellow candies in a pack, but not yellowy-green.

Dispersion – The measure of how spread out the data are. If there is very little dispersion, the data are closely grouped. Whereas if there is a high level of dispersion, then the data have a higher range.

Efficiency – The measure of the output per the amount input. An efficient process will provide results with little energy or resources devoted to it, but an inefficient process will require many resources for relatively few results.

Error – The probability that the results are due to chance and not the variable(s) being tested. There are many types and sources of error, some are within the control of the researcher and some are beyond, but quality research strives to record and discuss possible sources and consequences of error.

Estimate – The approximate value. An estimate assumes that the person making the estimate is familiar enough with the scenario to make an educated guess as to what the final value will be; the estimate.

Expected Value – The value that is predicted by experience or calculations. This value is not due to the result of the researcher's experimentation, but is based on theory.

Experiment – The test designed to assess the researcher's hypothesis.

Experimental Design – The experimental design is the plan to test the hypothesis that involves a treatment group and a control. Whether individuals are in the treatment or the control group is determined by the researcher's protocol, and the researcher can control the other factors to assess whether the independent variable does have an affect on the dependent variable.

Experimental Variable – This is another term for the independent variable in an experimental study.

Extraneous Variable – Like the confounding variable, this is anything not being tested that may affect the results. Extraneous variables may be controllable or beyond the control of the researcher, but the researcher should discuss possible impacts of these variables.

Fisher's Exact Test – This nonparametric test determines whether there is an association between two categorical variables. It can be used even if there are small samples as it uses matrices to calculate a critical value.

Fischer Least Significant Difference (LSD) – One of the post hoc analyses for an ANOVA, the Fischer LSD is the post hoc test most likely to show a statistical difference. In this way, it is the least stringent and has the greatest tendency to make a type one error.

Friedman Test – A nonparametric test that is parallel to the repeated measure ANOVA and is used to determine if a significant difference exists among three of more dependent groups.

Hypothesis Test – The protocol used to determine whether there is a significant conclusion to be drawn from data.

Homogeneity – The similarity of the variances between samples. Homogeneity is a measure of how similar the samples are to each other and to the overall population.

Independent Sample/Group – An independent sample or group has members that do not interact with or affect other samples or members of the population with respect to the measured characteristics.

Inferential Statistics – The numbers that allow a researcher to test a hypothesis and draw inferences about a population.

Inter-Quartile Range – This measure of dispersion is associated with the ordinal scale of measurement and describes the distribution of data.

Interval Scale – The level of measurement where the scale is evenly space and scores can be compared, but there is no absolute zero, so measurements on this scale can not be manipulated with multiplication or division.

Kolmogorov-Smirnov Test – This nonparametric test evaluates whether a sample distribution is significantly different than a theoretical distribution. This test can be applied to ordinal level data.

Kruskal-Wallis Test – This nonparametric test uses pooled ranks for three or more independent groups of ordinal level data.

Least Squares – This test evaluates a trend line and how far away from that trend line the actual data points lie.

Level of Significance – Synonymous with level of confidence, the level of significance is the measure of how much the researcher is willing to have attributed to chance alone. If a researcher sets the level of significance at 0.01, then the data must show that 99% of the time the result found would be due to the variable(s) tested, and only 1 time in a hundred could the result be due to chance.

Manipulated Variable – In an experimental protocol, the manipulated variable is an independent variable that the researcher creates; a variable that does not already exist.

Mann-Whitney Test – Sometimes referred to as the Mann Whitney U, is used to determine if there is a difference in the rankings of two independent groups.

Matched Samples – A type of dependent group where the researcher matches participants based on characteristics when evaluating a hypothesis.

Mean – The "average" of a sample or population. All the values are added and then the sum is divided by the number of values.

Median – The "middle" value of a sample or population. To determine the median, all the values are arranged in order and the middle value (if there is an odd number, or the average of the two middle numbers if it is an even number of values) is the median.

Mode – The value that appears most often. There could be more than one mode if more than one number appear most often.

Moderating Variable – A secondary independent variable that is identified because it may affect the relationship between the primary independent variable and the dependent variable.

Multiple Regression – This parametric technique assesses to what degree multiple independent variables affect a dependent variable. Like a correlation, the regression coefficients can range from -1 to 0 to +1. The higher the absolute value of the coefficient in the regression equation, the greater the relationship between the independent variable and the dependent variable.

Nominal Data – This level of measurement is the weakest of the four. Numbers are used as labels for classification or identification. This level of measurement does not permit mathematical operations with the actual data, just frequency comparisons.

Nondirectional Hypothesis – A nondirectional hypothesis states the nature of a relationship but not which group or which direction a relationship will favor or tend towards. A nondirectional hypothesis is often converted into a null hypothesis.

Nonparametric Tests – These tests are useful to make inferences about the sample being tested. Nonparametric tests can evaluate data like their parametric counterparts, but because the assumptions for the parametric counterparts can not be met, the conclusions can not be applied to the entire population.

Normal Distribution – A symmetrical distribution centered on the mean, median and mode. A normal distribution is one of the basic requirements for applying parametric tests to data.

Null Hypothesis – A hypothesis that specifies that there is no connection or difference between the tested variables. This is the hypothesis that is tested by statistical tests.

Observed Value – The value found using an experiment or test. It is found by the researcher and used to evaluate the sample.

One-tailed Test – A test that is only concerned with either the values above or below the critical value. This is used when testing a directional hypothesis.

One-way Analysis of Variance – A statistical test is used to determine if a significant difference exists among the means of three or more independent groups and one independent variable.

Ordinal Data – This scale of measurement gives more information than the nominal scale. The ordinal scale includes a ranking of information in some kind of order as well as the identification and classification of the data.

Outlier – A datum that does not seem to fit with the rest of the data. Outliers can skew a distribution or obscure a relationship. Each outlier should be investigated. If it can be explained the chosen test should be run both with and without the outlier, including the explanation for the outlier.

Paired Sample t-test – A parametric test to compare the means of two dependent groups.

Parameter – A numerical summary characteristic of the entire population.

Parametric Tests – A group of statistical tests that allow the researcher to draw inferences regarding the entire population. In order to use a parametric technique, the researcher must ensure that certain assumptions are not violated. The assumptions establish that the sample tested is representative of the entire population.

Pearson Product Moment Correlation Coefficient – This coefficient is a measure of how well correlated variables are. The closer the coefficient is to +1 or -1 the higher the correlation, and conversely, the nearer the value is to zero the smaller the correlation.

Population – A complete collection of anything a researcher wants to study.

Power of a Test – The power of a statistical test is the probability that the researcher will reject the null hypothesis when it should be rejected.

Predictor Variable – An independent variable in a non-experimental study.

Probability – The chance of getting a desired outcome out of all the possible outcomes, probabilities can be expressed as percents, fractions or ratios.

Probability Sampling – A category of sampling techniques in which selection is due to chance. Each member of the population or its subset has an equal chance or being selected.

Proportionate Stratified Random Sampling – This technique requires the researcher to measure the percentages of each subgroup, and then randomly select a sample that has the same proportions as the population it is designed to represent.

Purposive Sampling – A non-probability technique, this method limits the selected items to those that meet a certain criterion. While this limits how the results may be applied, it may be a useful technique to measure an otherwise difficult to target population.

P-Value – The probability that the results of a study are due to chance instead of the variable being tested. This is intertwined with alpha levels, level of significance and level of confidence. Depending on how it is being discussed, all of these can refer to the same thing, even though there are subtle differences. Commonly, the p-value is the value found after the data were analyzed, the level of significance/confidence was set before the data were analyzed and both refer to the likelihood of a type I error, the alpha level.

Quartile – A representation of one fourth of the data. When all the data are arranged in order, they can be divided up into quarters. Each of those quarters, or quartiles is labeled, with the middle two being set around the median. Quartiles are the basis for box and whisker plots of data.

Quota Sampling – Similar to proportionate stratified sampling, the population is divided into subgroups and the researcher randomly selects from subgroups until a predesignated quota of items from each subgroup are met. This is in an attempt to better represent the target population and reduce sampling error.

Random Sampling – This technique is the basis for probability sampling. All members of the population have an equal chance of being selected. There are many variations on this procedure to try to minimize sampling errors, or due to constraints on the researcher.

Random Variable – This is a numerical outcome of a statistical experiment. The individual values of the variable are random, and unpredictable, but the distribution of all the values is known.

Range – A measure of the difference between the highest value and the lowest value.

Representative Sampling – A sample chosen so the characteristics of the sample are the same as the population from which it was drawn.

Sample – A sample is a subgroup selected from and representative of the population of interest.

Sampling Error – The possibility that the sample selected from a population does not accurately reflect the characteristics of that population.

Scatter Plot – The graphical representation of individual data points. Scatter plots are most commonly used in looking for outliers, but are also useful in visualizing patterns in data to better analyze the results of statistical tests.

Scheffe Test – A post hoc analysis for use when a significant difference is found with a one-way ANOVA. The Scheffe Test is a more stringent analysis and is less likely to make a type one error, but it is also less powerful.

Selected Variable – In an experimental study, if the variable already exists, it is referred to as the selected variable.

Significance Level – The significance level is synonymous with the level of confidence. The level of significance is the level that the researcher is willing to accept is due to chance and no the variable being tested. If the researcher selects a 0.01 level of significance, then they will be rejecting the null hypothesis when there is a 99% chance that the results are due to what is being tested, and will accept a 1% probability of error.

Simple Random Sampling – This protocol requires that the researcher be able to define every part of the population and that every part of the population has an equal chance of being selected. The selection of one item does not affect the selection of any other item.

Skewed Distribution – A distribution that is not centered on the mean, median and mode. Either due to an uneven distribution overall or some outliers, the mean is different than the median and mode in the distribution.

Spearman Rank Correlation Coefficient – This is a nonparametric measure of how well variables are correlated. Instead of relying on a normal distribution of scores, the Spearman Rank Correlation Coefficient (ρ) can be used when the Pearson Product Moment Correlation Coefficient can not.

Standard Deviation – The measure of how widely spaced data are from the mean.

Standard Error – The confidence in the measure of the standard deviation, it is the standard deviation divided by the square root of the number in the sample. The larger the sample, the lower the error and thereby causing greater confidence in the measured standard deviation.

Statistic – A summary characteristic of a sample.

Statistical Inference – The generalization made based on sample data. The confidence of the inference is determined by the effects of sampling errors and the statistical tests employed to analyze sample data.

Stratified Random Sampling – The population is divided into subgroups and the sample is drawn from the subgroups. This technique is used to assure that subgroups are represented in the sample.

Survey Design – A data collection process using an instrument to obtain large amounts of relatively cursory information. Depending on the length and design of the instrument, the researcher may conduct follow up interviews or studies to collect more in-depth information. The amount and quality of information vary greatly by the length and depth of the instrument chosen, and the desired return rate.

Symmetry – The mirror image like quality of a distribution. A distribution with the same number and arrangement of values on either side of the middle.

Systematic Random Sampling – The method of choosing every nth element of a population for a sample. This procedure is at a greater risk for bias as compared to other random sampling techniques.

Target Population – The population about which inferences are to be made.

Test Statistic – The result of a statistical test that is then compared to a table of critical values or a p-value to determine whether the null hypothesis should be rejected.

Treatment – The way the researcher has manipulated the independent variable in an experimental study.

Tukey Honestly Significant Difference (HSD) – A post hoc test applied after a significant difference was found in a one-way ANOVA. This test falls in-between the Tukey LSD and the Scheffe tests as far as power and stringency.

Two-sample t-test – This form of the t-test is used to determine if a significant difference exists between the means of two different groups. This is the parametric alternative to the Mann Whitney U test.

Two-Stage Random Sampling – This technique is similar to the cluster random sampling technique. The researcher uses groups that are already defined, randomly selects from those groups and then applies another random technique to the selected group.

Two-Tailed Test – This requires using both ends of the distribution when analyzing data. Two tailed tests are used for both null and non-directional hypotheses.

Type I Error – The chance that the null is rejected when it should not have been. A significant difference or relationship was found when there was none. Sometimes called an alpha level, it is the probability that chance caused the result instead of the tested variables.

Type Two Error – The chance that the researcher fails to reject the null when it should have been rejected. No significant difference was found and it did exist. This type of error, beta error, is unknown and unknowable. As one increased the level of significance the likelihood of a type II error increases.

Unbiased Sample – A sample that accurately represents the population it was designed to represent.

Uniform Distribution – A distribution with a constant probability, either due to the variables being unrelated or too closely related. A uniform distribution looks like a flat line.

Variance – The square of the standard deviation. This is another measure of how widely spread data are.

Wilcoxon-Ranks Test – This nonparametric test is used to compare the distributions of ranks of two dependent groups.

Sources

ACITS, The University of Texas at Austin Statistical Services, (1997, July 31). Repeated Measures ANOVA Using SPSS MANOVA. Retrieved August 3, 2008, from http:// www.utexas.edu/cc/docs/stat38.html

Arkkelin, D. (n.d.). Using SPSS to Understand Research and Data Analysis, Electronic Version. Retrieved August 3, 2008 from Valparaiso University, Web site: http://wwwstage.valpo.edu/ other/dabook/toc.htm

Cooley, W. W. & P. R. Lohnes. (1971). Multivariate Data Analysis. Somerset, NJ: John Wiley & Sons, Inc.

UCLA: Academic Technology Services, Statistical Consulting Group. (2007). Introduction to SAS. Retrieved July 9, 2008 from http://www.ats.ucla.edu/stat/sas/notes2/

Johnson, R. (1996). Elementary Statistics. Belmont, CA: Wadsworth.

Morrison, D. F. (1967). Multivariate Statistical Methods. New York: McGraw-Hill.

Overall, J. E. & Klett, C. J. (1972). Applied Multivariate Analysis. New York: McGraw-Hill.

Roberts, M. J. & Riccardo, R. (1999). A Student's Guide to Analysis of Variance. London: Routledge.

Tabachnick, B. G. & Fidell, L. S. (1996). Using Multivariate Statistics. New York: Harper Collins College Publishers.

Thorne, B. M. & Geisen, J. M. (2003). Statistics for the behavioral sciences (4th ed.). New York: McGraw-Hill.

Weisstein, E. W. (2008). Variance. MathWorld--A Wolfram Web Resource. Retrieved September 12, 2008 from http://mathworld.wolfram.com/ Variance.html

Index

About the Authors

Dr. John W. Mulcahy is the Charles A. Dana Professor of Educational Leadership, Professor of Management and Senior Professor in the Schools of Business and Education at the University of Bridgeport. He has just completed his 40th. year in Higher Education and is the immediate past president of the National Academy for the Advancement of Educational Research.

This is Dr. Mulcahy's sixth book. He is the recipient of the LL.D.(h.c.), Johnson and Wales University and the D.H.L.(h.c.), Iona College. Dr. Mulcahy' degrees include: B.S., Fordham University, M.S. and M.B.A., Iona College and Ph.D. Fordham University.

Dr. Jess L. Gregory is a recent graduate of the University of Bridgeport's Doctoral Program in Educational Leadership, where she earned the award for the Outstanding Dissertation of the Year. Dr. Gregory is an urban educator devoted to making abstract concepts concrete.

A graduate of Dartmouth College, Dr. Gregory earned her A.B. in Classical Studies and, while teaching in both urban and suburban settings, was awarded an M.S. of Environmental Education.